GW01185565

HYDERABAD *hazir hai*

HYDERABAD
hazir hai

WRITINGS FROM THE
CITY OF NIZAMS

EDITED BY

VANAJA BANAGIRI

RUPA

Published by
Rupa Publications India Pvt. Ltd 2013
7/16, Ansari Road, Daryaganj
New Delhi 110002

Sales centres:
Allahabad Bengaluru Chennai
Hyderabad Jaipur Kathmandu
Kolkata Mumbai

Edition copyright © Rupa Publications India Pvt. Ltd 2008

Preface copyright © Vanaja Banagiri 2008

Copyright of individual pieces remain with the individual authors.

First published in hard cover in 2008.

ISBN: 978-81-291-2458-6

10 9 8 7 6 5 4 3 2 1

Typeset in Original Garamond by Mindways Design, New Delhi

Printed at Yash Printographics, Noida

Contents

Preface

❧

I remember vividly the scene when the seeds for this book were sown. My first book *Butterflies and Barbed Wires* had just been released. R K Mehra, the man responsible for my birth as an author, was in Hyderabad. He had invited me and a fellow author for dinner at the Taj Banjara. We were sitting by the lake, digging into kebabs, enjoying the breezy weather. RK said, 'The best part about Hyderabad is its food.' Even before he had completed the sentence, I jumped up and went on and on about how food was just one facet of Hyderabad. Undoubtedly most famous but other aspects like the jewellery, culture, lifestyles, Dakhni Urdu and most importantly the people, were all equally, if not more unique. 'You know,' I said with bursting pride, 'if anybody lives by the adage—If life gives you a lemon, make a lemonade—it's us Hyderabadis.' As I regained my breath from my self-indulgent hyperventilation, RK said, 'I smell a book there.' And I thought to myself, now I know why this man is one of the most sought after publishers in the country. He sees a book in anything that captures his imagination. Though I said it was a great idea, I must confess, I never really believed at that point that he actually meant it. It was more like a dinner table conversation that gets relegated to the recesses of one's memory and is sometimes even forgotten.

A week later I received a mail from him, which referred to our discussion of that night. 'I would like to know your thoughts on the subject,' it said. I was taken by surprise at the speed of his response and almost fell off my swinging chair as I read the mail. I suggested we do an anthology instead of my researching the city since we had enough and more stalwarts and authorities who were nothing short of living encyclopedias and also the ones who had experienced the charms of the Charminar city. RK loved the idea and before I could collect my thoughts, the contract landed in my post box promptly.

I got the message.

I was left with no time to drag my feet. I had to take the plunge right away. And that's exactly what I did. What followed was an exciting journey, Herculean at times, but exciting nevertheless. Exciting as tracing the journey of a city that has its origins in the richness of romance, wealth, culture to the bustling IT Mecca that it is today can't be anything but that. Which other city can boast of a name that is derived from a ruler's beloved? Quli Qutb Shah had originally named the city—Bhagyanagar—after his beloved Bhagmati and when she became his wife and changed her name to Hyder, he rechristened it as Hyderabad. Now, that's what we call royalty. And there lies the true mark of a romantic man. And that for us is Hyderabadi ethos. But before I lose the plot and get a tad carried away, let me get back to the anthology. Indeed, it was a formidable task because the writers I had zeroed in on were as elusive as the Hyderabadi punctuality. However, I must thank each one of them for tolerating me and entertaining my calls as well as my pestering emails (sometimes five in a day, no exaggeration!) at all odd hours.

My wild goose chase had its funny moments too. Like the time I ran into one of the anthology writers at a dinner. She waved a quick 'hi' from a distance and disappeared before I could get to her. Eventually, I tracked her and she said very sheepishly, 'I just realised the deadline for my article was yesterday when I saw you.' We had a good laugh over it.

And then there were amazing writers like Narendra Luther, who went out of his way to ensure that his piece reached me much before the promised date even though he had received my mail very late due to some cyber aberration. I would also like to mention Lakshmi Devi Raj who has been as endearing as the Hyderabadi *tehzeeb*, keeping the communication lines open 24x7 with not so much as a hint of irritation. And at her age, that is almost unreal. One day I kept sending her text messages and all she said when I finally called to check why she hadn't responded to any of my sms was 'beta, I don't know how to operate the sms. Please excuse me.' I can never forget how silly I felt in front of her humility despite her looming presence in all-important walks of Hyderabadi life. That, to me, is trademark Hyderabadi royalty minus the crown or the title. Her article gives us a peek into the life and times of Hyderabad that once was.

So what makes this anthology extra special? Yes, certainly the choice of our writers but more importantly, their choice of subjects. Like the typical *Hyderabadi Dastarkhan*—served to titillate every taste bud and satiate every palate—in true Hyderabadi *mehman nawazi* style, the contributors have handpicked every single spice to dish out this irresistible buffet.

Here are the people who have lent their very special touch to the banquet. Vijay Marur with his Hyderabadi wit treats us to side splitting tales; Vinita Pittie and her version of Hyderabadi adventure in the lingo; Syam Prasad Reddy's typical Hyderabadi enterprise of creating wealth; Iqbal Patni's poetic first person account of the Charminar tracing Mahboob Ali Pasha's life and times; Bakhtiar Dadabhoy's walk down the memory lane of the Salar Jungs and the famous namesake museum; Dinaz

Noria's first hand experience of lavish weddings, the big fat Hyderabadi wedding as she calls it; Shankar Krishnamurthy who is an outsider for all practical purposes gives us a ring side view of the hospitality business; Rani Sarma's fascinating account of the Deodis; Pratibha Karan's mouth-watering journey of the legendary Hyderabadi cuisine; Mohammad Ali Baig's rich legacy of theatre; Sangita Reddy's Apollo story; Dr Aminuddin Khan's nostalgic account; Fawad Tamkanat's kaleidoscopic view of Hyderabadi influence on his art and his special gesture of letting us use his work for the cover; Mithi Chinoy's fascinating account of Hyderabad Parsis; Syed Ali Zahir's historical account of Dakhni Urdu; G. Rajaraman's tribute to Hyderabadi sportsmanship.... Phew, I just realised what an exhaustive list that makes. So, what are we waiting for? *Aiye, Hyderabadi daawat haazir hai. Sirf aap ka lutf uthana baqi hai.*

Like the legendary Hyderabadi poet Maqdoom Mohiuddin once said of our city: '*Mohabbat baqi hain. Shehar ka nishaan abhi baqi hain.*' *Tasleem.*

Let the *wah wah* roll in.

Timeline of Hyderabad

Asif Shafuddin

The World	Period	Historical Event	Architectural Contribution & Cultural Event
	1 BC to AD 3	Satavahanas (North Deccan)	
	4 AD-5 AD	Vakatakas of Vidarbha	
	5 AD-6 AD	Vishnukundis of Andhra	
	c.556-757	Chalukyas of Vatapi (West & Central Deccan)	
	c. 630-970	Eastern Chalukyas of Vatapi (Andhra Pradesh)	
	c.753-973	Rashtrakutras (West & Central Deccan)	
	c. 973-1189	Chalukyas of Vatapi (West & Central Deccan)	
	c.1100-1327	Hoysalas of Dvarasamudra (West & Central Deccan)	
c. 1190-1294		Yadavas of Devagiri (North Deccan)	

The World	Period	Historical Event	Architectural Contribution & Cultural Event
	1310-1346	Khiljis and Tughlaq invasions	The invasions resulted in the ultimate decline of the three most important ruling dynasties and paved the way for the Vijaynagar kingdom in the Tungabhadra region and the Bahmani Kingdom in northern Deccan.
	1347-1526		Takes possession of Golconda Fort. During the reign of Sultan Mohammad Shah Bahmani (1358-1375) Raja Krishna Dev, a Kakatiya King of Warangal, handed over the mud fort, then called Mankal, to Muhammad Shah Bahani of Gulbarga under a pact.
Qutb Shahi Dynasty			
	1495	Sultan Quli Qutbul Mulk	High ranking Turkish officer made Subedar of Telengana. Sultan Quli made his head-quarters in Golconda. He strenghthened it with granite fortifications. According to legend the name Golconda was derived by combining the names of two of the sultans most loyal courtiers, Gulla and Kuntiah.
	1518	Qutb Shahi Dynasty founded	With the disintegration of the Bahmani Kingdom, Sultan Quli assumed independence and founded the Qutb Shahi Dynasty. At the age of ninety-nine he was killed by his son Jamsheed Quli. Sultan Quli built a massive citadel called Muhammadnagar, well known for its trade in diamonds and precious stones. Masjid Safa at Golconda is the first Qutb Shahi mosque of Hyderabad. Twenty five years later Sultan Quli was assassinated by Mir Mahmud Hamadani, Qiladar of Golconda at the instigation of the heir apparent Jamsheed Quli Qutb Shah.

Babur 1st Mughal Emperor of India	**1526**		
Humayun 2nd Mughal Emperor of India	**1530**		
Death of Guru Nanak	**1538**		
	1543	Jamsheed Quli Qutb Shah	Third son of Sultan Quli who ruled for seven years and died in 1550 of an incurable disease.
	1550	Subhan Quli Qutb Shah	Jamshed Quli's son was thrust upon the throne at the age of seven. After seven months his paternal Uncle Ibrahim Qutb Shah swept his nephew aside.
		Ibrahim Quli Qutb Shah	During his exile with the Raja of Vijayangar Ibrahim learnt to love Telugu. During his reign he patronised and encouraged the learning and writing of Telugu. Golconda was further streghthened.
Akbar 3rd Mughal Emperor of India	**1556**		
	1562	Husain Sagar (Tank Bund)	Built by the Sufi saint Husain Shah Wali (son-in-law to Ibrhaim Quli), on a tributary of the Musi River. It links the cities of Hyderabad and Secunderabad. There are two sarais (rest houses) on either side and four sluices to regulate the level of water in the tank.
	1578	Purana Pul Bridge completed	Built by Sutan Ibrahim Qutb Shah the bridge has 22 arches, is 600ft long, 35ft broad and 54ft above the river bed.
	1580	Muhammad Quli Qutb Shah	During Muhammad Quli's long, peaceful and prosperous reign

The World	Period	Historical Event	Architectural Contribution & Cultural Event
			the dynasty reached its zenith. Built the city of Hyderabad to accommodate the surplus population of Golconda. According to legend the King built it for the love of the beautiful Bhagmati whom he titled 'Hyder Maha'. The city was then named after her. 'Let millions of men and Women of all Castes, Creeds and Religions make it their Abode, Like Fish in the Ocean' – Prayer of Sultan Mohammed Quli Qutb Shah, while laying the foundations of Hyderabad. The fifth King planned Hyderabad as an 'open city'. It was to have no walls. The Qutb Shahis already had their well-fortified Golcnda Fort to fall back upon at times of need. Vajihi, an Urdu poet in his court wrote the famous work *Laila Majnu*
	1585	Mir Momin made Peshwa (PM)	Mir Momin came from Persia and was known for his learning, piety and poetry. He was an architect and lover of culture and associated with the layout of the city. At the steps of his mausoleum was buried the famous poet of Emperor Aurangzeb, Mirza Ahmed Niamath Khan Ali.
	1591	Charminar completed	Inadequacy of water, and frequent epidemics of plague and Cholera persuaded the fifth Quli Qutub Shahi ruler to venture outward to establish the new city with the Charminar at its centre and with four great roads fanning out in the four cardinal directions. Built during 1591-92 to a height of 56.7meters, on a square base of 31.5metres, Charminar

			is said to be a protype of Tazia, a representation of the tomb of Imam Husain
	1594	Badshahi Ashur Khana	
	1594	Charkana (Four Arches)	
	1595	Darush – Shifa (House of Cure)	
	1598	Jama Masjid	
Gunpowder Plot Jahanghir 4th Mogul Emperor of India	1605		
	1612	Sultan Muhammad Qutb Shah	Scholar, deeply religious and a connoisseur of good books.
	1617	Mecca Masjid	Sultan Muhammad Qutb Shah begun the building of the mosque which was completed seventy-seven years later by Aurangzeb.The largest mosque in Hyderabad, it is patterned on the Grand Mosque in Mecca under the direction of Daroga Mir Faizullah Baig and Choudhary Rangaih. The marble graves of the Asif Jahi rulers lie at the southern end.
		Sultan Nagar	
		The Qutb Shah Chronicles	
Voyage of the Mayflower	1620		
Charles I – King of England	1625	Daira Mir Momin	
	1626	Abdullah Qutb Shah	Ascended the throne at the age of twelve. The Kingdom was extended during his rule.

The World	Period	Historical Event	Architectural Contribution & Cultural Event
			Hayath Nagar Mosque built by Hayath Bakshi Begum. The mosque has five double arches and two minarets. The extensive courtyard is surrounded by several hundred double rooms known as 'Sarai of Ma Saheba' for the use of travellers. Within the courtyard lies the 'Hati Bauli' (Elephant Well) formerly drawn by elephants.
Taj Mahal	1631		In the royal palace of Hayath Nagar, was celebrated the first shave of the seventh King, Abdullah Qutb Shah for twelve days.
	1636	Hyderabad came under Mughal pressure	
	1645	Tavernier chronicled the diamond industry of Golconda	The Koh-i-noor was found in Kollur near the River Krishna in 1656.
	1656	Golconda attacked by Mughal army	
Aurangzeb 5th Mogul Emperor of India	1658-1707		
	1666	Hayath Bakshi Begum dies	Only daughter of the fifth King, wife of the sixth King and Mother of the seventh King.
			Ma Saheb Tank (1624), Husaini Alam, Bibi Ka Chasma, Langar, Hayath Nagar Mosque were all built in her memory. She also built the Khairatabad Mosque for her tutor Akhund Mulla Abdul Malik. Akhund built a tomb opposite the mosque which lies vacant as he died in Mecca.

| 1672 | Abul Hasan Tana Shah | Staunch defender against Mughal might. A benign and tolerant King. In 1687 he was taken prisoner by Aurangzeb and died after twelve years of captivity. Jan Sapar Khan, a noble of Aurangzeb was made govenor of Deccan.

Kalamkari, the art of textile painting flourished in a place called Masuilpatnam. Minature painting incorporated both Hindu and Islamic traditions resulting in the birth of a Deccani tradition. Abul Hasan granted a village, Kuchipudi, to a Brahim because he was good at presenting dance dramas. Today Kuchipudi is one of the important classical dance forms of India. |
| 1678 | Miyan Mishk Masjid | |
| 1684 | Syed Shah Raju II (Syed Shah Raziuddin) dies | Shah Raju was a nephew of Husain Shah Wali. Abul Hasan Tana Shah was his devoted disciple and built a splendid dome over his grave. |
| 1687 | Aurangzeb Mughal Army besiege Golconda | Under Aurangzeb's ambitions to expand the Mughal Empire, Chin Qalich Khan led an attack into the Deccan and later died from his wounds. After eight months of trying to penetrate the sturdy walls and territory of Golconda, Abdullah Khan Pani treacherously opened one of the gates (Fateh Darwaza) to let in the Mughal invaders.

Azhdaha Paikur Gun used during the siege of Golconda by Aurangzeb's army lies on the Musa Burj, southeast of Golconda Fort. Fateh Maidan is where Aurangzeb pitched his first |

The World	Period	Historical Event	Architectural Contribution & Cultural Event
			camp on his victorious campaign against Golconda.
	1694	Mecca Masjid completed	
	1699	End of Qutb Shahi Kings Advent of Mughal Rule	Mubrez Khan was the last Mughal Subedar. City wall and gates built during Mughal rule
		Asif Jahi Dynasty Mir Qamaruddin's new title 'Chin Fateh Khan'	
Farruksiyar, Mogul Emperor	1713-1719	Mir Qamaruddin new title 'Nizam-ul-Mulk Fateh Jung'	Farruksiyar conferred on Mir Qamaruddin the tiltle of Nizam-ul-Mulk Fateh Jung (Regulator of the Realm).
	1724	Nizam-ul-Mulk given the title of Asif Jah declares independence	While the Subedar of Malwa at the Delhi court secretly instructed Mubrez Khan, the Subedar of Deccan to oppose him, Mubrez Khan was defeated in battle and established Asif Jah's supremacy in the Deccan. Aurangabad becomes the capital of the State. Hyderabad Dominion expanded by waging a struggle against the Marathas and by the policy of non-involvement in the rivalry for power between the British and the French.
	1756	French enter Hyderabad	The French forces entered Hyderabad in order to install an Asaf Jahi Ruler of their choice. In the end it was the choice of the British that prevailed. Meanwhile in 1756, French General Monsieur Bussy had occupied the Charminar for a few days.

George III King of England	**1760**		
	1763	Nizam Ali Khan	Second Nizam Ali Khan ascended the throne. He ruled for forty-one years and employed the French adventurer Monsieur Raymond.
Captain James Cook expedition to Australia	**1768**		
	1769	Hyderabad becomes capital of the State	
	1803	Sikander Jah	Third Nizam ruled for twenty-six years and appointed Mir Alam as his Prime Minister who was responsible for maintaining good relations with the British.
			End of the war with the Marathas.
			Secunderabad was named after the third Nizam. Originally established as a cantonment after 1798 when a subsidiary alliance for military and political cooperation was signed between the Nizam and the British East India company.
	1809	Munir-ul-Mulk appointed Prime Minister	Munir was the son of Mir Alam. William Palmer & Co, a banking house introduced in Hyderabad by the British. Due to overspending and heavy borrowing from the bank the finances of the State were in a bad shape.
French Conquests of Algeria	**1829**	Nasir-ud-Duala	Fourth Nizam ruled for twenty-eight years.
	1830		
	1846	Church of the Holy Trinity Built	The Church was built with a contribution from the private purse of Queen Victoria.

The World	Period	Historical Event	Architectural Contribution & Cultural Event
	1853	Salar Jung appoined PM	Salar Jung brought about several reforms to improve the finances of the Dominion.
	1857	Afzal-ud-Daula	Fifth Nizam ruled for twelve years. Afzal Gurj Bridge Afzal Gurj Mosque
	1869	Mir Mahboob Ali Khan	Sixth Nizam ascended the throne at the age of three and ruled for forty-two years. AKA Mahboob Ali Pasha he was installed on the masnad by the British Resident and Sir Salar Jung, who also acted as the co-regent.
Queen Victoria declared Empress of India	1876		
	1883	Salar Jung dies	
	1893	Urdu official language	Persian was the official language up to 1893 and then Urdu up to 1948.
	1908	Floods wash away city wall.	
	1911	Mir Osman Ali Khan	Seventh Nizam ruled for thirty-seven years. Made Honorary Lt. General of the British Army. Elevated by King George V from 'His Highness' to 'His Exalted Highness'. Title of 'Faithful Ally of the British Government' was conferred on him. A 21-gun salute signalled his arrival in Britain (Other rulers were only entitled to 19-guns). He led a simple life but was one of the richest men in the world.
India gained Independence and Partition	1947		

1948	Hyderabad State merged with the Indian Union	
	Operation Polo (Police Action)	
1956	Hyderabad becomes capital of Andhra Pradesh	On 1 November 1956 the map of India was redrawn into linguistic states
1967	Seventh Nizam dies	

Dakhni Language

Ali Zahir

South India has many classical languages but there is a special language which was and still is the link language of the South called Dakhni language. This language came into existence probably in the thirteenth century when the North Indian forces of Allauddin Khilji (1296–1316) invaded South India for a brief period. Later on Mohammad bin Tuglaq (1325–1351), the ruler at Delhi, thought that the central location of Devagiri (near Aurangabad) was more appropriate to rule his expanded kingdom. Hence he shifted his capital from Delhi to Devagiri in the year 1327, later renaming it as Daulatabad, but due to geo-social reasons (as the sovereign ordered all the respected citizens of Delhi to shift) the plan failed and soon he had to return to Delhi. This adventure may have been a disaster in socio-economic terms but it certainly enriched the newly developing Indian language known as Dakhni, Hindavi, Gujari, etc. The thousands of poor Delhites who could not afford to return to their city and stayed back in Deccan further contributed towards the proliferation of the language since their interaction with the southern population was through Dakhni.

Of all the independent kingdoms that arose on the ruins of the Delhi Sultanate, the Bahmani kingdom of the Deccan proved to be the most powerful. It came into existence during the reign of Mohammad bin Tuglaq, challenging his authority. The nobles of the Deccan driven to rebellion by the eccentric policies of the Delhi Sultan seized the fort of Daulatabad and proclaimed Ismail Mukh, the Afghan, as king of the Deccan under the title of Nasiruddin Shah. However, he being an old and laidback man, proved unfit to effectively rule such a large kingdom. So he soon voluntarily made room for a more worthy leader Hasan, entitled Zafar Khan who was declared king by the nobles on 3 August 1347. He assumed the title of Abul Muzaffar Alauddin Bahman Shah but was popularly known as Hasan Gangu Bahman Shah.

The Bahmani Period lasted from AD 1347 to 1525. In the beginning the capital of the Bahmani kingdom was at Gulbarga but in the later years it was shifted to Bidar. Both these places are now in Karnataka. This era added a wealth of Dakhni culture in the form of architecture, literature, painting, music, dance and cuisines. But perhaps its most precious gift was the Dakhni language which is still spoken in the regions south of Vindhya mountains.

The Bahmani kingdom was spread from the Arabian Sea in the west to the Bay of Bengal in the east and from the Vindhya Mountains in the north to the Tamilnad in the south. Dakhni served as the link language for the people of this vast area. The places where this language flourished were Gulbarga, Bidar, Ahmed Nagar, Golconda, Bijapur, Karnool, Caddappa, Vellore, Chennai Patan (Chennai), Bodhan, and Aurangabad.

The rulers of Bahmani Kingdom were great patrons of poetry and literature so much so that in the year 1390 the Sultan of the kingdom Muhammad Shah II invited the famous poet of Iran, Hafiz of Shiraz, to Deccan. Hafiz accepted the offer, went up to the island port of Hurmuz in southern Iran but had to abandon his journey due to the turbulent waters of the Gulf.

After the fall of the Bahmani kingdom in the early sixteenth century, five independent sovereign states were formed. Two of them, the Adil Shahi in Karnataka and Qutub Shahi in Andhra, are significant for their contribution towards the development of the Dakhni language and culture. These two neighbouring states were ruled by just and broadminded rulers who patronised Dakhni and Persian besides other languages. As a result, many significant and famous works of literature in Telugu, Kannada, Dakhni and Persian were written in these kingdoms during the sixteenth and seventeenth centuries. In the late seventeenth century these kingdoms were conquered by the Mughal Emperor Aurangazeb after which the North Indian language called Hinadavi, Reekhta or simply Hindi, which is now identified as Urdu, became the official language in the region. Thereafter, proper Dakhni started getting less precedence in the literary circles. But the spoken language very much remained as Dakhni.

The cycle of the development of Dakhni language which was heralded by the coming of the North Indian forces in the thirteenth century to the South ended with the North Indian forces again occupying the Dakhni Sultanates in the seventeenth century. Though Dakhni remained as a spoken language but as far as its literature is concerned it dried out subsequently. Hence in course of time a language was reduced to just a dialect and in later centuries very little of importance was written in Dakhni.

The famous linguist and Urdu scholar Syed Mohiuddin Qadri Zore considers the period of literary Dakhni language to last from AD 1350 to 1750. He indicates the period from AD 1580 to 1672 as the zenith of Dakhni. The fall or disintegration as described by him in his book *The History of Deccani Language* started from 1672 and went on till 1687. But I think that the real downfall of Dakhni happened after 1687 when both the Bijapur and Golconda kingdoms were annexed by the Mughals.

However the period when Ibrahim Adil Shah (1580-1626) ruled over Bijapur and Mohammad Quli Qutub Shah (1580-1611) controlled Golconda was the golden period for Dakhni literature. Both these kings themselves were good poets of this language besides being great patrons of art and literature. They not only encouraged their own language but also did significant work for the promotion of regional languages like Telugu and Kannada along with classical languages like Persian, Arabic and Sanskrit. Ibrahim Adil Shah wrote his masterpiece on Hindustani music called *Naw Rass* which deals with ragas and raginis of Hindustani music. Similarly, Mohammad Quli Qutub Shah's work on Dakhni poetry called *Diwan-e-Quli Qutub Shah* is so far considered as the first complete book of poetry in Dakhni as well as in mainstream Urdu. Apart from the kings themselves, their courts too could boast of great poets like Nusrati, Wajhi and Jaanam. All these poets find a place of eminence in the history of Urdu literature.

Wajhi wrote his famous work of fiction called *Sabras* in Dakhni prose, a very interesting story of beauty, heart, mind and love. The story is woven around the characters named after these parts of the human body. Mind is an emperor; Heart is his son; Beauty is a princess of another country and her father is another mighty emperor Love. Now this lady Beauty has the Abe Hayat (water of life) in her possession. Prince Heart goes in search of the Abe Hayat and encounters all sorts of very interesting adventures. Of course he falls in love with princess Beauty. *Sabras* though a work of fiction has numerous allegorical connotations of Sufi thought. This story is still popular and has been published in several forms. It marks a seminal contribution to popular Dakhni fiction.

The famous historian of medieval Indian history Mohammad Qasim Firishta graced the court of Ibrahim Adil Shah and was commissioned by Ibrahim Adil Shah to write the well-known book *Tareekh-e-Firishta*. This book is a great source of reference for all modern Indian historical studies even today.

It is interesting to note that the famous poet Vali Aurangabadi went to Delhi from Deccan in the year AD 1700 when Aurangazeb was still alive. He met his spiritual mentor Hazrat Shah Saadullah Gulshan who advised Vali to write poetry in 'Reekhta' meaning a mixed language which was the Urdu of those days. He took the advice seriously and started writing poetry in the language which is closest to the modern day Urdu. His poetry inspired the North Indian poets of the day and they too began composing poetry in the spoken language rather than Persian which was the language of the elite. This way the Dakhni which owed its existence to North Indian influence gave back a much developed language to the North in the form of Urdu. It was Urdu which consequently produced timeless poets like Mir Taqi Mir and Mirza Ghalib in the subsequent centuries.

Unfortunately, due to the military conquests of the North Indian Mughal armies, Dakhni became a language of the defeated, being ridiculed and thereon considered as a lesser medium of expression by the new ruling class. Hence an unseen but strong socio- political pressure compelled Dakhni people to use Urdu as the standard written language in place of Dakhni. This is also the reason we hardly find any work of significance written in Dakhni after the fall of Bijapur in 1686 and Hyderabad (Golconda) in 1687. As a result, Dakhni gradually lost its position as a standard literary language. With the passing of time this wonderful language became just a dialect of mainstream North Indian Urdu.

AS far as Indian cinema is concerned, with some rare exceptions, the Dakhni language has been used in various commercial movies for making people laugh. Poetry also has been written in this language by many humour writers for light entertainment and jest. However, no serious work of literature or art has been produced in Dakhni in the last four centuries. Now after a long hiatus, it is interesting to see Dakhni being used seriously without any hesitation as a creative language. The screenplays of two successful Hindi movies which were recently made in Hyderabad—*Angrez* and *Adab Hyderabad*—had the entire screenplay written in Dakhni. These movies also proved that Dakhni is not only appropriate for comic scenes but also for intense, serious drama. Earlier in the year 1971 a play called *Adrak ke Panjey* was staged by an unknown playwright and stage actor Babban Khan. This play was in Dakhni and it ran to packed houses for almost thirty years in different parts of the world.

It is the democratic spirit of India which I feel is giving hope for the return of the Dakhni as a mainstream language. I believe the time is ripe for the revival of Dakhni. There remains no one standard language now. The hegemony of the aristocratic upper classes of princely India in defining culture is a thing of the past. Now Dakhni can no longer be marginalised or ignored as there is a considerable population of people which wants to use it to express their feelings and ideas. It is very much alive as a spoken language in many parts of South India. I hope that novels and serious poetry too will appear in this language and help it gain the place of prominence that it deserves.

Hyderabadi Roots

Aminuddin Khan

My father was old enough to be my grandfather. He was born in Hyderabad in 1880, the second son of his parents. Scion of an old noble family, he grew up in the shadow of his elder brother, and like him was educated by a team of tutors. He spoke Urdu, Persian and English fluently. As my grandfather insisted that his children learn to speak Telugu, Marathi and Kannada also—the family jagirs being scattered across the Nizam's Dominions—Father spoke the three major southern languages too, and like a native. He was also very proud of the fact that his forbears, who first settled in North India, had built a citadel in Narnaul. The Marwari patois was prevalent in the region in those days and his family had quickly familiarised itself with the language. Interestingly, it was part of everyday life in our Machli Kaman deodi in the Old City till the twentieth century.

At the age of twenty-one my father, Ghiasuddin Khan, married Jeelani Begum of Mangalaram. She was distantly related and considered a most suitable match. She was an only child and, in due course, inherited a vast estate.

I was told that Jeelani Begum, of Afghan stock, was almost six feet tall. My father was five feet and six inches in socks. There is not a single photograph of the two of them standing together. She is invariably seated on a chair with him standing upright beside her. But it is supposed to have been a good, blissful marriage; except for one sad reason. She had eleven children, not one of whom lived to be a year old. She died a few hours after the last child was born.

My father was distraught, so much so that a few months after her demise he walked out of the deodi and headed for the Himalayas. Five years later, he was sighted in the courtyard of Ali Ahmed Sabir's dargah at Kaliyar, a tiny village on the banks of the Ganges, near Roorkee. As soon as the news reached Hyderabad, a deputation consisting of his younger brother, eldest sister and three cousins, rushed to Kailyar and persuaded him to come back home. His elder brother had died in a polo accident during my father's absence and the family needed him to take his place.

A year later, my father married the girl who was to become my mother. She was the youngest daughter of the Subedar of Gulbarga, and just under twenty when she married him. He was almost fifty. If Jeelani Begum's firstborn had survived, she would probably have been as old as my mother.

Despite the age difference, my maternal grandmother, a widow by then, did not hesitate to give my mother, Kazimunnisa Begum, in marriage to a much older man. In fact, this is the strategy she adopted with all her daughters. They were married off, in turn, to rich, aristocratic, well settled, respected widowers with children from previous marriages.

My mother had a miscarriage during her first pregnancy, which convinced my father that the old pattern was establishing itself again. But I was born a year and a half later, in 1932. Father had an enormously elaborate celebration for my first birthday. The party lasted from morning to night. There were three thousand guests, coming and going, the women in the zenana, the men outside. Meals were served throughout the day and entertainment was provided by troupes of dancing girls and singers. Old-timers still talk about the party. I have a photograph of that one year old boy, adorned like the Sultan of Turkey, wearing an embroidered fez cap, dripping with jewellery, propped beside his mother, who is hugely pregnant. Exactly a week later, she died of a ruptured uterus, leaving my baby sister behind.

Needless to say, the Nawab was devastated, once again. But this time it was not possible to set off for the Himalayas, leaving two little children behind. Happily, there were two women he could rely on to help him with their upbringing. One was my chachi, Qaiseri Begum, wife of Father's younger brother. The other was Barbara Walsh, a young English lady who came out as a companion for my mother during the first year of her marriage, and stayed on as my governess. I called my aunt 'Mummy' and Miss Walsh 'Washy' and am beholden to them for what they turned me into by the time I was seven.

My father died in 1939 a few days after the Second World War broke out in Europe. Even before his remains were interred, my maternal grandmother had petitioned H.E.H the Nizam of Hyderabad to have me removed from the house in which I lived. She convinced the Nizam that if I was left in the charge of my uncle and aunt I would be poisoned within a week! Why the Nizam agreed with her suggestion I don't know. But at eleven o'clock that night he sent the Director of the Court of Wards to pick me up.

I was put into one of H.E.H's Humbers, the Director beside me, and close to midnight, handed over to Miss Grace Linnell, the Principal of the exclusive Mahbubia Girls School. She already had three Court of Wards' girls living with her, but

I was the first boy she was to take on. A little later my sister arrived from Towli Chowki, where she had spent the whole day with my grandmother. It was very difficult to explain to a sleepy six year old why we were in a strange villa in the middle of the night and why Daddy didn't come and pick us up. Why didn't we telephone and ask him?

My sister lived with Miss Linnell till she was married. Like her, I went to the Mahbubia Girls School for a year. In 1941, Miss Linnell took me to Dehra Dun and handed me over to Miss Hersilia Oliphant who had started the Welham Preparatory School for Indian Boys a few years earlier. The decision to shift me to a residential school was taken by the Nizam in consultation with the senior member of the State's Executive Council, a British officer belonging to the Indian Civil Service. I spent two years at Welham and five at the Doon School.

I used to come home during the school holidays twice a year and go back twice a year, always by the Grand Trunk Express. Home was where Miss Linnell and my sister happened to be. Miss Linnell became my surrogate mother. Few people have impacted me the way she did. For my sister, I became more than an elder sibling. To this day I am her father-mother substitute.

The first thing I had to do on arriving in Hyderabad was to go and see the Nizam of Hyderabad at Nazri Bagh in King Kothi Palace, and show him my term report. He was always puzzled that I did not do well in maths. But he was caring and genuinely curious about how I was doing at school. He also had a wry sense of humour that I enjoyed hugely. He had known me since I was a small boy. My father used to take me to see him quite often. So he was not a stranger. I had always been frightened by his reputation, but gradually got to love him so much that when I heard—over the radio—that he had died, I put my head between my knees and sobbed like a child. That was in 1967. I was married by then, with two children of my own, living in the hills of Kerala.

The turbulent years from 1942 to 1948 coincide with my schooling. I became conscious of the geo-political change that was brewing in India because I spent most of the year in a province of British India. If I had been schooled in Hyderabad, it is doubtful if I would have been even half as aware of what was going on in the country. I was still at Welham School when Sir Stafford Cripps came to India as the head of a commission. He was here to discuss the possibility of independence for the Indian people. Cripps proposed that the country be divided into two sections, one for Muslims and the other for Hindus. He also raised the hopes of the Indian princes who began to dream of their own independence. The proposal was to lead to Mahatma Gandhi's call for 'Quit India'.

The repercussions in Hyderabad were mixed. Some wanted British rule to end, some were uncertain of the consequences, and some felt that if Independence came it would prove to be disastrous. I often wondered what my father would have had to say had he been alive. Hyderabad was an island cut off from the mainstream of Indian politics. It had its own currency, coins, postal stamps, army, railway, police force and civil service. Its people were insular. The aristocracy and other vested interests were unwilling to change the shape of things. The State was governed by a council of ministers headed by a President, who eventually came to be known as the Prime Minister. The ministers were not public men, but officials who had risen by stages to cabinet rank. The Prime Minister reported to the Nizam. He was the biggest and the richest of the Indian princes, convinced that his status was unquestionable, that he had a special relationship with the British government and that the government of India was fully aware of it, his dynasty having held sway over a large part of the Deccan for 200 years. But, the rub was obvious. He was a Muslim ruler of a State that was predominantly Hindu.

The Indian National Congress was opposed to the Nizam's rule. However, as the 1942-1945 years coincided with the Second World War, little changed in the State of Hyderabad. The Nizam picked his Prime Ministers, kept in close touch with the British Resident, contributed heavily to the war effort, and carried on as if it would all work out in his favour in the end. It was not to be. By 1946 the demand for Pakistan had become vehement. Partition followed in 1947 and the British cleared out of the country in unseemly haste—a whole year before the scheduled date they had set—leaving an unholy mess behind. The lives of millions, on both sides of the new international border, were horribly disrupted.

In Hyderabad a new factor had come into being: a revisionist movement headed by Qasim Rizvi, a small town lawyer. He claimed that Hyderabad belonged to the Muslims and the Nizam was their representative, honour bound to rule on behalf of his co-religionists! The rank and file of Rizvi's movement was called Razakar. Although efforts were made by Rizvi to turn his followers into a homogenous body through a semblance of military training, they were no more than an undisciplined mob. The Nizam had no sympathy for the Razakars. But gradually, by threats, bullying, making inflammatory speeches, and arming his followers, Rizvi pushed the Nizam into a corner and he became a 'prisoner in King Kothi Palace', no longer in direct touch with actual happenings in the State. However, Rizvi evidently had an agenda of his own. He wanted independence for Hyderabad State, on par with India and Pakistan, firmly underwritten by the British Crown!

Mr M.A. Jinnah met the Nizam at the time and is supposed to have called the idea a 'pipe dream'. His Exalted Highness was not amused. He did not like anybody casting aspersions on the eminence of his dynasty. Mr Jinnah advised the Nizam to join the Indian Union in due course and not even think about possible affiliation with Pakistan, when it came into being.

As long as the British protection was available in India, the Nizam felt relatively comfortable, but when they withdrew he was faced with a situation he was least prepared for. The result was disastrous. Any person or party that could please him most, made him swing in their direction. He seemed to have no opinions of his own any longer. Some of the closest members of his inner circle were obviously not giving him an objective picture of where he stood. On the other hand, certain loyal well-wishers, liberal in outlook, always had a sobering effect on him. So did Sir Walter Monckton, his Constitutional Advisor and Lord Louis Mountbatten, then Viceroy of India. Soon negotiations began. An Indian Agent General was posted in Hyderabad and a Hyderabadi Agent in New Delhi. The former occupied the erstwhile British Residency in Bolarum, the latter lived in Hyderabad House in the capital. But progress was slow. Qasim Rizvi did not like what was happening and sabotaged the delicate process. He went to Delhi to see Sardar Patel and the Indian government to acquaint them of his point of view. Nobody of importance gave him an interview or took interest in him. He came back furious, determined to create friction between Hyderabad and the Government of India.

In one of his infamous speeches, Rizvi said that the flag of the Asaf Jahs would soon fly on the ramparts of the Red Fort. The Razakars openly declared that they would depose the Nizam if he did not comply with their wishes. The Nizam appointed Mir Laik Ali to head a new Rizvi approved government. That was the beginning of the end. There was a popular uprising in the border districts against the high-handed behaviour of the Razakars, and an economic blockade of the State by the Union Government. Not long afterwards, the Police Action brought about the fall of the Nizam, the end of his 225-year-old dynasty, the arrest of the Prime Minister and Rizvi, and the collapse of the feudal structure of Hyderabad.

In September 1948, from one of the terraces of my maternal grandmother's house at Towli Chowki, I watched a flank of the Indian Army drive into the city along the Bombay road: tanks, armoured cars, troop carriers, trucks and Jeeps. My mother's eldest sister was dabbing her cheeks with the end of her sari. 'Our lives will never be the same again,' she said.

From the age of eleven I had never been able to understand why her generation expected Hyderabad to remain unchanged forever. I recalled what my father had often said in my presence: 'Duniya fani hai, mian (The world is transitory, nothing lasts).' He was right, of course, but what a pity it was, I thought, that Hyderabad had come to such an inglorious end.

Today, by a twist of fate, I am the Administrator of H.E.H the Nizam's Private Estate. I have an office in the Nazri Bagh area of King Kothi Palace, which was the private residence of the Nizam. Once in a while I go and sit on the verandah where he used to sit in his rickety cane chair, read, make notes on a white washed pillar to his right, chat and meet people informally. I think of the boy who came to see him from time to time. I recall the Nizam's figures of speech, his cackle, and his chain smoking habit. But I never leave the verandah feeling sad. In fact, thinking of the old man cheers me up and makes me laugh.

Three Salar Jungs and a Museum

Bakhtiar K. Dadabhoy

The name Salar Jung is a famous one, at least in Hyderabad, if not the whole of India. In the main, this fame attaches due to the enormous and magnificent collection of curios, antiques, and *objets d'art* which is associated with the name of Yousuf Ali Khan, better known as Salar Jung III. He is also the best remembered of the three diwans of Hyderabad who bore the title of Salar Jung. What is generally less well-known is that his grandfather, Sir Salar Jung I, was the greatest diwan Hyderabad ever had. And the collection for which Salar Jung III, the 'Great Collector', gets almost all the credit was started by Salar Jung I, the 'Great Diwan'. In fact two of the most famous pieces in the Salar Jung Museum were acquired by Salar Jung I. Sandwiched between the 'Great Diwan' and the 'Great Collector' is Salar Jung II, a fleeting character on the political stage, as indeed, on the stage of life itself. His claim to fame lies mainly in being the son of a famous father, and the father of a famous son.

The purpose of this article is twofold: firstly, to briefly tell the story of the three Salar Jungs; and secondly, to narrate how private enthusiasm and individual exertion became a source of enjoyment and instruction on the arts, to so many others. We will trace how a heterogeneous accumulation of objects, which had struck an avid collector's fancy on his travels in India and abroad, became an orderly presentation of a selection based on significance and quality. The old order yielded to the new, but it also bequeathed a rich legacy for succeeding generations to treasure and enjoy.

The Heritage

The Salar Jungs were the direct descendents of Ali Zaman Hyderyar Khan, Munir-ul-Mulk, who was the diwan of Hyderabad from 1809-1832. Munir-ul-Mulk had married Nafisa Begum and Sahiba Begum, daughters of Mir Alam, the diwan, who was a descendent of the Nuria Sayids of Iran. In 1803 the Nizam, Asaf Jah III, appointed Mir Alam, whose real name was Mir Abul Qasim, as his diwan. Mir Alam was succeeded as diwan by his son-in-law, Munir-ul-Mulk, in 1809. Munir-ul-Mulk was an inept administrator. A dummy diwan, the real power vested with his Peshkar, Raja Chandulal, a Punjabi khatri, who was a favourite of the English. Munir-ul-Mulk remained diwan till his death in 1832, after which Chandulal, long the de facto diwan, was formally appointed to the post, which he held till 1842.

With Sahiba Begum, Munir-ul Mulk had two sons, Muhammed Ali Khan, Shuja-ud-Daula and Alam Ali Khan, Siraj-ul-Mulk, who was diwan from 1846-48, and again from 1851-53. The eldest son, Shuja-ud-Daula, married the daughter of Saiyid Qasim Ali Khan Bahadur, a nobleman. Turab Ali Khan, (the future Salar Jung I), the offspring of this union, was born on 2 January 1829. It was also the year in which the Nizam died. He was succeeded by Nasir-ud Daula, who became the fourth Nizam. By now the British stranglehold on Hyderabad was complete. The Resident had an important say in the appointment of the diwan. The diwans were beholden to him and ensured that British interests were well protected.

The period 1842-1853 saw the vacillating Nizam appoint as many as six diwans—three of whom had tenures which ranged from two to five months. Munir-ul-Mulk's other son through Sahiba Begum, Siraj-ul-Mulk, was first appointed as diwan in 1846. He was replaced by Saif Jung in 1848. In 1851, when the British pushed the Nizam he was obliged to appoint him once more to that post. Siraj-ul-Mulk was a man of great learning and did not covet the post of diwan. It was during his tenure that Berar was ceded to the British, and given his partiality to the British, was blamed by both the Nizam and the populace, for the loss. Deeply disturbed by all the happenings, Siraj-ul-Mulk passed away only three days after the cession.

Salar Jung I

Turab Ali Khan was descended from diwans on both sides of his parents. He was a grandson of Munir-ul-Mulk, and a great grandson of Mir Alam, both of whom had held the post of diwan. Unfortunately, his father, Shuja-ud-Daulah, died just two years after his birth. Young Turab was brought up by his uncle Siraj-ul-Mulk with all tenderness and care, and was never allowed to feel the absence of a father. As a child he had a weak constitution and his health remained delicate till his twelfth year. His education and training were in keeping with the requirements of a boy of his social standing. In 1841, he was given the title of Salar Jung Bahadur. His public life started in 1847 when he was appointed taluqdar of Khammam district by his uncle who was the diwan. A year later the responsibility of managing the family jagirs was entrusted to him. He managed them efficiently, and in 1853 inherited them on the death of his uncle. His interactions with his uncle also groomed him indirectly in state craft, and his administrative skills improved with experience.

The Young Diwan

When Siraj-ul-Mulk, his uncle, the diwan, died in May 1853, Turab was installed in his place on 31 May 1853 by the Nizam, Nasir-ud-Daula, Asaf Jah IV, in a public durbar at the Chowmahalla palace. At the young age of twenty-four, Turab found himself occupying a post of great power and responsibility. This was a happy day for both Turab (henceforth Salar Jung I) and Hyderabad, for the history of Hyderabad during his long tenure of thirty years (1853-1883) as diwan is little more than the history of Salar Jung I's reforms. Salar Jung I's reform of the medieval oligarchy that was Hyderabad, took many forms. Limitations of space prevent us from delineating them in detail but the following paragraphs provide the flavour.

When the young diwan assumed office, the government was in deep debt to all sorts of creditors. The sahukars gave loans to the government at extortionate rates. The cession of Berar compounded the problem because people who held jagirs there wanted to be compensated for their loss. The salaries of the Nizam's relatives could not be paid for want of funds. To top it all, the Nizam was clamouring for the release of his jewels which had been pledged in England to repay part of the state debt. Collection of land revenue was farmed out to people on a commission basis. Another pernicious aspect of the prevailing system was collection of land revenue in kind. The nobles did nothing but live off the land and the people. They had vast jagirs and were subject to no law. The Arabs, the Rohilla, and the Sikh mercenary bands constituted the other power centres. The Arabs did not acknowledge the jurisdiction of the local, civil, and criminal law or authority. Commerce and banking were controlled by the sahukars who often took the assistance of the mercenaries to realise their dues. Unsurprisingly, the state did nothing to further the cause of education or public health.

Early Reforms

Salar Jung I, during his tenure at Khammam, had seen the beneficent effects of the English 'settling' the land revenue as against collection on a commission basis. He resolved to transform the existing system along English lines. Since this major change would affect many vested interests (including the Nizam), he took the express permission of the Nizam before launching his reforms. He promised regular payments to the Nizam and his dependents. In return he asked to be given a free hand in dealing with corrupt and inefficient officials. A treasurer guilty of defalcation was dismissed and imprisoned.

Salar Jung I also banned the practice of nazrana—a gift to the appointing authority, including the Nizam—for a job. He voluntarily cut his own salary and also cut the salary of his Peshkar. To set an example he married a widow with the celebrations being very low-key. He also refused to accept any gifts on the occasion. His reduction in salaries was accompanied by a promise of regular payments. This reform worked wonders and the markets became buoyant. Salar Jung I's reform earned him the gratitude of not only the salaried class, but also of the petty traders.

The Great Administrator

Salar Jung I's reforms were interrupted for a while. The Nizam, Nasir-ud-Daula, died on 17 May 1857. His son ascended the throne under the title Afzal-ud-Daula. A week before, the sepoy mutiny had taken place in Meerut. The sneeze in Meerut threatened to give Hyderabad a cold. But Salar Jung I and the new Nizam, Afzal-ud-Daula, resolutely sided with the British and the incipient uprising met an ignominious end. The grateful British government gave presents to both the Nizam and Salar Jung I. They returned the districts of Raichur, Doab and Naldurg, and gave Sholapur to the Nizam. A debt of rupees five million was written off. (The Nizam not to be outdone reciprocated with gifts worth fifteen thousand pounds to the Governor-General.) This effusion of gratitude was fully deserved: had Hyderabad fallen, the words of the Governor of Bombay's telegram to the Resident may well have become a grim reality: 'If Hyderabad goes, everything goes.' In 1861, a new order—the Star of India— was instituted and it was conferred on the Nizam.

Having earned the gratitude of the English, Salar Jung I felt free to continue his reforms that were interrupted by the mutiny. He abolished the system of farming out the collection of land revenue to others and the payment of land revenue in kind. Instead, he adopted a pattern where a 'settlement' was fixed for thirty years and where improvement in yield attracted no additional levy. He abolished some petty taxes and introduced new ones like the stamp duty, excise, customs and road tax. Examining the state debt he found that the claims of the sahukars were exaggerated to the tune of eight million rupees. He paid off the Pathan and Arab creditors and got fresh loans for the balance from the sahukars who were impressed by his earnestness in paying off the state debt. Thereafter he put down the armed might of the Arabs, Pathans and the Rohillas. He also got the Arabs to acknowledge the authority of the common courts.

By 1864 Salar Jung I's basic reforms were in place. The state's revenue had tripled and its indebtedness had decreased drastically. A collector was appointed in each district with revenue, civil and magisterial powers. Separate treasuries were established in each district, and the departments of police, health and education were set up. A Board of Revenue was also established at this time.

In the next phase, Salar Jung I divided the state into five divisions and districts. Since as diwan he could not leave

Hyderabad without the express permission of the Nizam, inspections were carried out by divisional commissioners. He also created four posts of assistant ministers (drawn from the nobility) to assist him in his duties. Salar Jung I also established regular courts of justice and made the judiciary independent. It is largely due to his efforts that the rule of law was established in Hyderabad. A large number of schools were set up, including the famous *Madarsa-e-Aliya* (The Exalted School) for the education of the nobles' children, including his own sons. He also encouraged female education and educated his daughters on western lines.

On the communications front an electric telegraph system was introduced for official purposes. A regular postal system was established in 1862. The Railways followed, thanks to Salar Jung I coaxing the Nizam into agreeing to the proposals made by the Government of India, who favoured the railways for both commercial and strategic reasons. The Nizam was opposed to the idea because he feared that the attendant openness would endanger orthodoxy. Salar Jung I's efforts did not go unrecognised. In 1867 he was invested with the insignia of the Knight Commander of the Star of India. Four years later he was created a Knight Grand Commander of the Most Exalted Star of India (K.G.C.I).

Salar Jung I's most important administrative reform however came in 1882, just a year before his death. He created five ministries with a total of forty-four departments under them. The ministries were assisted by a permanent secretariat and he invited a number of suitable persons from other parts of India to fill important posts. He took the advice of Sir Syed Ahmed Khan in his selection of suitable persons. The seeds of modern government as we know it today were sown by Salar Jung I who despite an adversarial relationship with the Nizam (who held his family responsible for the loss of Berar), and constant intriguing at court, managed to transform, in the words of the Governor-General Lord Metcalfe, 'a creaky, corrupt, medieval oligarchy into a modern working machine in which the rule of law was introduced'. On one occasion, Afzal-ud-Daula, the Nizam, insulted Salar Jung I in open court. Salar Jung I resigned; the Nizam was forced to eat humble pie. Salar Jung I emerged from the exchange with greater powers. Salar Jung I also had the English to thank for his success. The Resident had made it clear to the Nizam that he could not remove the diwan without the permission of the Viceroy. Whenever Salar Jung I found the Nizam blocking him he threatened to resign, fully aware of the impotence of the Nizam in this regard.

Apart from the Nizam, Salar Jung I also had trouble with the Paigah nobles. Strangely, Salar Jung I also had his share of trouble with the English. After the death of the fifth Nizam, serious differences arose between the Resident and Salar Jung I who was co-regent. And the Berar issue was always present in the background, souring relations. Things became so bad that Lord Lytton, the Governor-General, wrote to Lord Salisbury, the secretary of state, in September 1877, that Salar Jung I was 'the most dangerous man in all India; and like a horse, or a woman that had once turned vicious, thoroughly irreconcilable'. Obviously, cosying up with the English was now a thing of the past.

In 1876 Salar Jung I visited England at the invitation of the Duke of Sutherland. He travelled from Bombay to Naples, and subsequently went to Rome where he met Victor Emmanuel, the King of Italy. Later he had an audience with Pope Pius IX at the Vatican. It was during this trip that Salar Jung I acquired two of the most famous pieces in the Salar Jung Museum: *Veiled Rebecca* and the wood carving *Mephistopheles and Marguerite*. Salar Jung I also visited Paris. The visit, however, was an ill-starred one. He fell from the stairs of the Grand Hotel and sustained a painful thigh injury which he bore with characteristic fortitude and good cheer. In England he was received by the Duke of Sutherland at Folkestone. Oxford University gave him an honorary degree and he was also honoured with the 'Freedom of the City of London', the first minister of an Indian state to be so honoured. (The first Indian to be so honoured was Sir Jamsetjee Jejeebhoy, the first baronet, in 1855.)

Salar Jung I was a tall man with a broad build. He sported a moustache but shaved his head. He was punctilious about court etiquette and could never be faulted in his manners even before the child-Nizam Mahboob Ali Khan. He was also a lavish entertainer and a good host.

The 'Great Diwan' passed away on 8 February 1883 after a short illness. The cause of death was said to be cholera but his French governess swore that he had been poisoned. Thoughts of his own mortality appeared to have never been far from his mind. Whenever Salar Jung I went on a long trip he carried with him all the material required for a funeral should he pass away during the course of the journey. He was also conversant with astrology and may well have realised that his end would come when it did.

Salar Jung II

Salar Jung I had two sons and two daughters. Of his two sons, Mir Laik Ali Khan and Mir Sadat Ali Khan, it was the elder, Mir Laik Ali Khan, who ultimately succeeded him as diwan. When Salar Jung I died, the Nizam had yet to attain the age of majority. A council of Regency was formed with Mir Laik Ali Khan as secretary to the council. Both he, and Maharaja Narendra Bahadur, his father's old friend, were appointed as joint administrators for the purposes of day-to-day administration.

Mir Laik Ali Khan was born on 13 November 1861, and was educated first at home, and then at the *Madarsa-e-Aliya*, where he was a pupil till 1882. He along with his brother was sent to England for higher education. He was a keen sportsman, a splendid shot, and a good billiards and lawn tennis player. A highly intelligent man, he was an excellent speaker, and had a very good memory. However, he was indecisive and also inexperienced.

At a durbar held in October 1883 he was given the title of Salar Jung, thus becoming Salar Jung II. On 5 February 1884 when Mahboob Ali Khan was formally installed on the *masnad* by Lord Ripon he was made diwan of Hyderabad. It was a logical choice. Laik Ali Khan was the son of Salar Jung I, a class fellow, and a boon companion of the Nizam. His accession to the post of diwan was marked by great warmth and for a while the Nizam and his diwan shared the most cordial relations.

However, it did not take Laik Ali Khan long to make himself extremely unpopular with his sovereign. The Nizam felt terribly slighted by the breach of court etiquette of which Laik was routinely guilty. Laik forgot that there is a wide gulf which separates a commoner from a prince, and presumed too much about his friendship with the Nizam. His impudent familiarity even prompted the Nizam to say, 'He did not consider me equal in rank, but lower.' The relationship turned very sour often prompting harsh criticism from the Nizam. Unsurprisingly, he was dismissed in April 1887, despite having the support of the English. Salar Jung II had made some superficial administrative changes in his short tenure of three years. The change from Persian to Urdu as the official language took place when he was diwan, and the seeds of a 'Mohammedan University' were sown by him even though the Osmania University was established at the time of the seventh Nizam, Mir Osman Ali Khan.

Salar Jung II went on a European tour in 1887. He was honoured with the K.C.I.E. by Queen Victoria. He returned to India in 1889 but passed way in Poona on 7 July 1889 at the young age of twenty-seven. It is said that he died of a broken heart. It was not the loss of his position that grieved him as much as the condition imposed on him to seek permission to enter Hyderabad.

Salar Jung III

When Salar Jung II died, his son, Yousuf Ali Khan, the future Salar Jung III (who was born on 13 June 1889) was only twenty-four days old. His widow returned to Hyderabad with her infant son. Yousuf grew up under the watchful eyes of his mother and a few faithful retainers. His health, like that of his grandfather, was delicate in the early part of his life. The Nizam, Mahboob Ali Khan, did not allow his differences with the infant's father, Salar Jung II, to affect his relationship with the child. He took the child under his personal care and protection and gave special attention to his education. Private tutors were appointed to teach him. He also attended the *Madarsa-e-Aliya*. The Nizam was given regular reports about his progress, and even the Government of India was kept informed about the education of the young child through the Resident.

Yousuf Ali Khan was a bright child, even though he continued his studies at home and did not study in a college. A bibliophile, he was one of the most widely read nobles of Hyderabad. The physical side of Salar Jung III's development was also given special attention. After the early phase of delicate health, he regularly played cricket, football and tennis. He had his own cricket team, in which he also played along with Nawab Moin-ud-Daula. He became a good swimmer despite the fact that he nearly drowned at the age of five. He liked riding, tent-pegging, and polo. He had his own polo team (the Salar Jung Polo Team), owning fifty to sixty polo ponies.

Since Yousuf had lost both his father and his uncle by the time he was one year old the estate was looked after by Salar

Jung I's mother. On her death in 1895 the estate was handed over to a committee appointed by a royal mandate. Since the Nizam was unhappy with the functioning of the committee, the management of the estate was entrusted to Raja Lalta Pershad, and the then Revenue Secretary, A. J. Dunlop. Since the estate was deeply in debt the Nizam paid off half the debt from his personal finances.

In 1898, on the occasion of the Nizam's birthday, Yousuf was conferred with the titles of Khan, Bahadur, and Salar Jung. He was also given a *mansab* of two thousand five hundred, cavalry of one thousand five hundred, *alam* (flag) and *naqqara* (kettle-drum). When Mahboob Ali Khan passed away in 1911, Salar Jung III mourned his death the way he would that of a blood relative. Mir Osman Ali Khan became the seventh Nizam, and it was during his reign that Salar Jung III was invested with full powers to administer his estate comprising 1480 sq. miles and a population of nearly two lakh people.

When Raja Kishan Prasad Bahadur, the diwan, resigned in 1912 citing health grounds, the Nizam decided to appoint Salar Jung III in his stead. His appointment was received with unconcealed delight by the people of Hyderabad. Given his qualities of head and heart it was expected that he would at least equal, if not outshine, his worthy grandfather. But fate decreed otherwise. History repeated itself when he resigned in 1914 after only two and a half years, due to personal differences with the Nizam.

His mother who had seen a similar fate befall her husband, and witnessed the tragedy of his early demise, was naturally worried about her son. A depressed Salar Jung III was referred to the family physician Dr Hunt for treatment. That worthy gentleman, having no modern drugs at his disposal, made the suggestion, that perhaps, Salar Jung III should amuse himself like the European nobility by collecting art objects. This struck a receptive chord in the young Nawab. The loss of premiership was put at the back of his mind, and in time, modern India gained a magnificent collection of art objects.

Salar Jung III however did accomplish some notable tasks during his short tenure as diwan. It was in his time that the Department of Archaeology and a Small Causes Court were set up. A large number of scholarships were given to deserving students for studies both in India and abroad. He also contributed his own money to this end. Like his father, Salar Jung III also travelled to England and the Continent after he resigned as diwan. In February 1921 he returned after a stay of many months laden with rare objects and numerous books. Again, in May 1927 he left for England. On his return he followed this up with trips to Japan and the Middle East.

Salar Jung III was of fair complexion, medium height and lean build. He had a high-bridged prominent nose and a broad forehead. He sported a thin moustache. Of dignified deportment he was a man of graceful manners, fine intellect and extraordinary memory. He also had a capacity for business. Shaking off the prejudices of his class he became a practical man of business, becoming a director of a number of companies, and also investing judiciously in some of them. He liked to dress well and favoured mauve coloured *achkans*, each of which cost no less than five thousand rupees.

How then, it may be asked, did such a man remain a bachelor? The story goes that his mother did not approve his marrying one of his cousins with whom he had been infatuated from an early age. He was then attracted to the daughter of the English Resident but political reasons prevented such a match. There was also talk of his interest in a number of other ladies from different communities but nothing came of it. The closest he came to marrying was when he was engaged to Leila Wellinker, (whose second husband was the famous filmmaker David Lean), but the engagement was cancelled. Others believe that Salar Jung III was far too self-centred to marry, and in all probability was not serious about tying the knot.

Salar Jung III's palace was a centre of culture. He also entertained frequently, generally favouring formal lunch parties. He himself ate sparingly. Even though he was a religious man he was tolerant of other religions and believed in communal harmony. He was, however, fond of the good things of life. He smoked; he drank, and maintained a fleet of cars. His cars were engraved with the words 'My trust is in God'. He invented a new cap called the 'Salar Jung cap' which became very popular in Hyderabad. He was a Freemason and besides collecting curios, books and manuscripts was a patron of poets, writers, and artists. He encouraged various literary, cultural and social activities and was also instrumental in the publication of many books on his family members. His own desire for confidential expansion found expression in his autobiography *Yousuf-e-Deccan*. He was a member of the Secunderabad Club and a number of books in his enormous library bear its stamp, presumably bought by him from sales of old books organised by the club. (The building of the club was donated by his grandfather Sir Salar Jung I).

Salar Jung III was a born connoisseur and aesthete. From his childhood he showed an interest in collecting art objects, no doubt influenced by the existing collection and the family tradition started by his grandfather, and continued by his father. He had inherited the *Veiled Rebecca*, the wood carving *Mephistopheles and Marguerite*, priceless oriental manuscripts of the Koran, and an illustrated anthology of Muhammed Quli, among other items. Salar Jung III added to these and over the years built a huge collection which filled his palaces. Whenever he purchased items which were small in size, he exhibited them on a round marble table in his Deodi. Anyone who evinced an interest in the pieces was shown not only those pieces, but also the famous *Veiled Rebecca*. Over the years, the collection assumed alarming proportions. His city palace and his country mansion at Saroornagar were full to overflowing with art objects. He knew the value of each piece in his collection and kept a vigilant eye on their preservation and location. It is said that he knew exactly where each piece had been stored or exhibited.

Salar Jung III's collection was the result of not only his travels in India and abroad, but also from purchases made on his behalf by agents of auction houses. Art dealers from all around the world sent him catalogues and kept him abreast of the new pieces available with them. Christie's and Sotheby's sent him their catalogues; Salar Jung III besides having agents in the principal Indian cities also used to participate in auctions in Hyderabad. J. Moosa, Rahim Khan and Abdul Aziz, the owners of the local auction halls, became his agents. His favourite jeweller in Bombay was Guzder who helped him evaluate foreign jewellery. Once he bought an entire mansion in Poona called 'Glad Hust' just to acquire its glass and porcelain collection. His collection boasted of Jehangir's wine cup and Aurangzeb's dagger, to mention only two objects in his enormous collection.

Salar Jung III's fame as a collector was so great that families selling their heirlooms gave him the right of first refusal. A kind hearted man he sometimes allowed himself to be duped because 'the man needed the money'. He was an expert in judging calligraphy and could identify the handwriting of any great writer of the past. His knowledge of paintings was exceptional, and he could identify the country of origin of a carpet by simply looking at the stitching and knots.

Salar Jung III had plans to set up a museum either at Khwaja Pahadi near the Mir Alam Tank or at Maula Ali. For a time, Poona and Ooty were also considered as locations. He spent a lot of time, energy and resources on the designs, but unfortunately death claimed him suddenly on 2 March 1949, before work could commence. His last purchase—a set of ivory chairs gifted to Tipu Sultan by Louis XVI—arrived after his death. But Salar Jung III had done enough to ensure that posterity would remember him forever. The Military Governor declared a public holiday as a mark of respect, and the Hyderabad Art Society convened a meeting and passed a resolution of condolence. The Society also resolved to start a museum associated with his name.

Private Passion to Public Pleasure: The Development of the Museum

In the beginning

Salar Jung III left behind more than 40,000 art objects, and a large number of books and manuscripts. The example of duty has often been set to the government by individual effort and private enthusiasm; and the government, which is almost always a tardy learner, has warmed to its task by slow degrees. In this case, however, it acted with some alacrity. Since Salar Jung III was a bachelor, the Government of India appointed a committee by virtue of a special ordinance to administer the affairs of the Salar Jung Estate. M.K. Velodi, the then Chief Civil Administrator of Hyderabad, approached Dr James Cousins, a well known art-critic, to organise the various objects into a museum. Since Cousins was engaged he suggested the name of G. Venkatachalam. The venue of the proposed museum was to be the Diwan Deodi, the ancestral palace of the Salar Jungs, and Salar Jung III's residence when he was alive. This newly born museum was controlled by the Salar Jung Estate Committee. The museum was declared open to the public on 16 December 1951 by Pandit Jawaharlal Nehru.

Since Salar Jung III had no direct heirs, his property had to be divided among a large number of his relations. There were 114

The Salar Jung Museum

claimants to the property who formed themselves into different groups and filed five different compromise memoranda in the court between 1956 and 1958. The Government of India and the Government of Andhra Pradesh passed a decree on 5 March 1958 considering all these compromise memoranda. By virtue of the Compromise Deed dated 2 December 1958 and the High Court Decree thereon, all parties to the suit agreed to relinquish their rights in all art objects and books in the museum and library in favour of the Government of India. The Compromise Deed was largely an outcome of the patience and diligence of Nawab Mehdi Nawaz Jung, chairman of the Salar Jung Estate Committee.

The museum then came to be administered by the Government of India as a subordinate office under the then Ministry of Scientific Research and Cultural Affairs. This arrangement continued till 1 July 1961, when the administration of the museum was transferred to the Salar Jung Museum

Board—an autonomous body formed by an Act of Parliament. On 1 July 1961, the Salar Jung Museum together with its library was declared to be an institution of national importance by an Act of Parliament known as the Salar Jung Museum Act, dated 19 May 1961. Under the Act, the Government of India vested the ownership of the collections and transferred the administration of the museum and library to a Board of Trustees consisting of eleven members, (five *ex-officio*, and six nominated) with the Governor of Andhra Pradesh as its *ex-officio* chairman.

Being autonomous, the Board is self-governing. However, the Government of India has retained powers to exercise overall control over the museum in matters pertaining to policy and finances. The Salar Jung museum has a unique status insofar that it is the only museum in India which is fully autonomous but is wholly financed by the Government of India. The Board is assisted by two important committees, the executive committee and the finance committee, which have been constituted for the administration of the museum. The museum prepares a budget which is presented to the Ministry of Culture. Since the museum does not generate enough revenue for all its activities, the shortfall is made good by grants-in-aid from the Government of India. The budget for 2006-07 was approximately Rs 14.6 crore. From 2.07 lakh visitors and ticket sales of Rs. 1.88 lakh in 1961-62, the museum was visited by 11.2 lakh visitors in 2006-07, generating revenues of Rs 1.2 crores.

A modern museum is born

The collection was earlier housed in the Diwan Deodi where the Oriental and the Western collections were displayed in seventy-seven rooms of the residential palace of the late Salar Jung III. (The Deodi was demolished about thirty years ago. The City Civil Courts are located in the area now.) However, for a variety of reasons, the Diwan Deodi could never have become the collection's permanent home. Accordingly, a master plan for the construction of a new building was submitted and it was decided to take up the work in three phases. The estimated cost of the project was Rs 97.05 lakh. The first phase was to construct a central block with the remaining two blocks, one on each side, to be taken up at a later stage. The bulk of the expenditure was to be borne by the Government of India, through the State Government.

The Salar Jung Estate Committee donated 5.8 acres of land situated on the southern bank of the Musi river and rupees five lakh. A piece of land measuring 4.75 acres was purchased and added to the plot donated, thereby making sufficient provision for the future expansion of the museum. The State Government provided a grant of five lakh rupees and also consented to construct the building through its Public Works Department. In view of the high cost, it was decided to proceed with the construction in a phased manner. The corner-stone of the new building was laid by Pandit Nehru on 23 July 1963. The central block of the new building was completed on 16 January 1968 at a cost of Rs 38.46 lakh. All care was taken in shifting the museum to its new home with the creation of a special post for supervising the move.

The library was the first section to be shifted. It was declared open on 15 May 1968. The work of shifting and rearranging was done simultaneously and the museum was opened to the public on 1 June 1968. It was officially inaugurated on 24 July 1968 by Dr Zakir Husain, the then President of India.

Since the old building lacked proper storage facilities, a large number of objects were on display making the galleries overcrowded. As a first step, duplicates and objects of secondary importance were sorted out. The objects on display have now been systematically classified and displayed. In view of the vast collection it was proposed to construct two more blocks on either side of the existing building. These two blocks, namely,

Turab Ali Khan Bhavan (Western Block) and Laik Ali Khan Bhavan (Eastern Bloc) came up in 1999. The plan is to ultimately house all the Western art in the Turab Ali Khan Bhavan and all the Eastern art in the Laik Ali Khan Bhavan. The central block will exhibit the entire Indian collection.

At present there are thirty-nine galleries in the museum in three blocks: the Indian Block (thirty galleries), the Western Block (seven galleries) and the Eastern Block (two galleries) in which 13,404 objects are on display. (This is a little more than about a fourth of the collection. Most museums display only a certain percentage of the objects in their possession. The Salar Jung museum is no exception—there are a large number of chandeliers and exquisite period furniture, among other artifacts, still waiting to be displayed.) The galleries of the museum are undergoing reorganisation, and the famous *Veiled Rebecca* has been relocated to a new gallery. The new galleries which have recently opened have modern, state-of-the-art lighting. The exhibition hall in the Turab Ali Khan Bhavan, named after the late Abbas Yaar Jung, a descendent of the Salar Jungs, and a former member of the museum's board for many years, was inaugurated by the Governor of Andhra Pradesh in October 2007. Plans for building a second floor in the Turab Ali Khan Bhavan are also afoot. There is also a founders' gallery where the portraits and personal belongings of the family attempt to recreate for the viewer, the life and times of the Salar Jungs. The second floor of the Indian block houses the library. The third floor is utilised for administrative offices and for the conservation laboratory, photography and engineering sections.

The museum has a director at its head. He is assisted by a joint director. The curatorial staff consists of keepers, deputy keepers, and gallery assistants. Their main function is to ensure safe custody of the artifacts both on display and in the stores, their documentation, maintenance of galleries and the reserve collection. Keepers are responsible for organising exhibitions and looking after gallery arrangement. Besides, there is also a photography section. Guide lecturers conduct tours for the visitors explaining the origin and importance of the objects on display.

The museum also has an Education Section which consists of four branches: Education, Documentation, Public Relations and Publications. The functions of these four branches include organising annual events, exhibitions, lectures and seminars; preparation of index cards and master ledgers; provision of guide services; and printing of guide books, catalogues, and other brochures and pamphlets.

The Chemical Conservation Wing plays a very crucial role in protecting the precious artifacts from damage and decay. The museum also has a preservation unit. An Engineering Wing was established in 1994 to supervise the execution of both civil and electrical works, and maintain the buildings and gardens. Presently it is associated in the ongoing project of re-organisation of the galleries.

The museum has also been acquiring art objects to augment the existing collection and fill gaps in the evolutionary sequence. It has also received gifts from various sources. Pandit Nehru gifted a diamond studded watch and Padmaja Naidu made a bequest comprising paintings, porcelain, furniture and bronze pieces in September 1976. The museum has also played host to the exhibition of the Nizam's jewellery.

The Collection

The exhibits of the museum can be broadly divided into Indian art, Persian art, Nepalese and Tibetan art, Sino-Japanese art and Western art. We will briefly discuss each in the following paragraphs.

INDIAN ART

Miniature paintings

The museum has a rich and varied collection of miniature paintings. These range from leaves of Jain-Kalpasutras, Mughal miniatures belonging to the reigns of Akbar, Jehangir and Shah Jehan, and the Deccani School of miniatures. The Salar Jung museum has one of the richest collections of early illustrated manuscripts of the Deccan under one roof. It also has a sizeable collection of Rajasthani paintings along with paintings belonging to the Basholi, Pahari and Kangra schools.

Modern Indian paintings

Among the exhibits acquired by the museum, modern Indian paintings constitute a large number. Though the beginning was made by Salar Jung III, the vast majority were acquired by the museum after 1962. They include works by Raja Ravi Varma, Abanindranath Tagore, Nandlal Bose, A.R Chugtai, Benode Bihari Mukherjee, Gopal Ghose, K.H. Ara, M.F. Husain, K.K. Hebbar and N.S. Bendre among others. The museum also boasts a good collection of graphics. There are intaglios by D.L.N. Reddy, Laxman Goud and Krishna Reddy, and lithographs by Tyeb Mehta, V.S. Gaitonde, M.A. Karim and others.

The bronze collection

The bronzes number about two hundred and include a Jain image of the eighth century and a Vishnu image of the late Pallavas dateable to AD 900. There are Chola bronzes and some Nataraja images. Bronze images of the Vijayanagar and Naik period also form part of the collection. Other items include temple implements like bells and decorative chains, incense burners and lamps, and a large variety of nut-crackers.

The textile collection

The textile collection of the museum is also a rich and varied one. The exhibits include Kashmiri shawls, tie and die Bandini work, Benares sarees, brocades and Jamdanis from Lucknow and Benares, Baluchar textiles, phulkari embroidery from Punjab, textiles from the Kangra valley, Chamba rumals, embroidery work from Kutch and Kathiawar, kalamkari textiles, Golconda cotton paintings and picchwais and brocade work. The museum also has a good collection of Telia rumals, Pochampalli rumals and patolas from Gujarat.

The ivory collection

The museum has a fine collection of ivory carvings from different parts of the world. The word ivory includes the tusks and teeth of the walrus, Narwhal, and the hippopotamus, apart from the elephant. The collection includes figures of humans and animals, chessmen, paper cutters, fans, carved boxes, book corners, bedsteads and much more. The chessmen and the *chausar* sets form an interesting group. A famous exhibit is the ivory mat where the threads are made of ivory.

The jade collection

The Salar Jung museum has arguably the best collection of jade in the country. Most of the Indian jade is carved with traditional floral designs. Many are also studded with precious stones. The objects consist of wine cups, *huqqa* pipe ends, plates, cups, belt buckles, book stands, arm rests, dagger hilts, archer's thumb guards, rings, jars, pots, bowls, hair pins and the like. Most of the objects belong to the Mughal and the later Mughal periods. The famous pieces of historical value include daggers belonging to Jehangir, Noor Jehan and Aurangzeb. There are as many as 130 jade handled daggers which are the most distinctive objects of Mughal jade.

Arms and armour

This collection has an amazing variety and quantity of old arms as well as firearms. There are more than 1,200 objects of armoury in the museum; the firearms number 196 and include match-lock, flint-lock, and muzzle loading guns, duelling pistols, revolvers, blunderbusses and cannons of different shapes and sizes. There are also swords, daggers, battle-axes, spears, maces, bows and arrows, shields, chest plates, helmets, and suits of armour in an incredible variety of shapes, sizes, material, decoration and techniques right from the sixteenth down to the twentieth century. The collection not only includes variants from India but also from Persia, Turkey, England, France, Spain, Germany, Nepal, Burma and Japan. The notable historical personages represented through the arms are Jehangir, Akbar, Shah Jahan and Aurangzeb. There are also two swords belonging to the Qutub Shahi period.

Miscellaneous pieces

Apart from the above there are also a large number of decorative pieces of silver filigree from Karimnagar and Cuttack, enamel work on gold, bidri ware, walnut furniture, and wood carvings. The museum also has lacquer coated *palkhis* and sedan chairs, sandalwood work, wooden chairs and stools inlaid with ivory and mother-of-pearl, Nirmal toys fashioned out of light puniki wood, Kondapally toys and miniature replicas of Dravidian temples made in sola pith, unrivalled for their detailed accuracy.

PERSIAN ART COLLECTION

The museum has a large collection of art objects from Persia in different media ranging from the seventeenth to the twentieth century. These comprise carpets, porcelain, metal ware, glass, enamel, textiles and paintings.

The museum has over 150 Persian carpets with a rich variety of floral, bird and animal designs. The museum has carpets from Bokhara including an unusual double sided carpet. Other Persian objects include porcelain tiles, wine bottles, rose water sprinklers, decanters, and scent bottles made of glass. There is also some beautiful metalware consisting of plates, mirror stands, trays, jars and ewers.

NEPALESE, TIBETAN AND BURMESE COLLECTIONS

The Nepalese art consists of some superb copper and bronze sculptures, temple lamps, snuff bottles, *khukris*, and spice boxes. The Tibetan collection is a small one and comprises a few *tankas* (scroll paintings) and large copper tea pots. The Burmese art in the museum shows the influence of Buddhism as well as that of the Hindu epics. There are some fine examples of wooden sculpture, Burmese lacquer work, temple gongs and dinner gongs.

SINO-JAPANESE COLLECTION

Though not acclaimed for its Sino-Japanese collection, the Salar Jung museum is one of the few museums in the country which can boast of a fairly extensive collection of Chinese and Japanese art. In all, there are more than 5,000 exhibits.

Chinese collection

There are more than 300 exhibits of Celadon ware, the earliest porcelain which reached the rest of the world. There are a few pieces belonging to the Ming period in this collection. The Blue and White collection assignable to the period of Wan Li consists of mainly jars and plates. Other groups include Famille Verte and Famille Rose, the latter taking its name from the opaque ruby pink enamel derived from gold which dominates the colour scheme in these pieces. Other exhibits include figures of the Buddha and Bodhisattvas in white ware called Blanc de chine. There are also a large number of snuff bottles in porcelain, jade, ivory and glass. The enamel ware includes painted enamels and a few examples of cloisonné ware of the Ming and Ching periods. There are also a wide variety of lacquered boxes and a few examples of lacquered screens. The rest of the Chinese collection has fine silk embroideries, a few bronzes and some exquisite carved jade objects.

Japanese collection

The Japanese collection consists of pieces of Arita, Imari, Hirado, Seto, Kutani and Satsuma porcelain. The cloisonné enamels mainly comprise vases and trays. There are woodcuts, water colour paintings, silk embroideries, lacquer work, and carvings in ivory. The museum also has a good collection of Japanese miniature sculptures called netsukes. There are also a remarkable collection of swords and daggers, including Samurai swords with ivory sheaths, representing the Katana (large sword) and the Wakizashi (small sword).

EUROPEAN ART

Paintings

European painting features prominently in the Western art collection in the museum. Works by English, Italian and French artists decorate the walls of the museum. The English artists include works by the nature painters J.M.W. Turner and John Constable. The classical style is represented by Sir Frederick Leighton, G. F. Watts, Sir Edward Poynter, among others. Animal painting of a high quality was achieved by Sir Edwin

Landseer and Thomas Sydney Cooper, both of whose works are represented in the museum. Of the Italian painters the most famous is Canaletto whose *Piazza San Marco* is in the museum's collection. Among French paintings, the pride of place goes to the immense still life by Jean Baptiste Simeon Chardin.

Sculpture

There are a number of marble statues in the museum, but the majority are garden figures. Of the original works, *Veiled Rebecca* by the Italian sculptor G. B. Benzoni, is the most famous. Carved from a single marble slab the Jewess Rebecca stands enveloped in a transparent veil, with all the contours of her figure finished with exquisite precision and clarity. It was acquired by Salar Jung I during his visit to Rome in 1876. There are also a number of copies of famous sculptures in the museum, the best known being copies of works by Antonio Canova and Giovanni Bernini. The most famous wood carving is the nineteenth century *Methistopheles and Marguerite* in French Sycamore wood, portraying a double statue in the neo-classical style, by an artist whose name remains unknown. It is also the only statue carved in wood available in the museum. This piece is displayed in the European paintings gallery. The bronze statues which include mythological subjects, historical and literary figures as their subjects, are almost all copies.

Porcelain, glass, and clocks

The porcelain collection includes Sevres pieces from France and Dresden from Germany. There are a good number of original Sevres pieces which can be dated to the reign of Louis XV, XVI and Napoleon I. The collection of Dresden porcelain is second in importance only to that of Sevres and there a large number of fine pieces in the collection. English porcelain is represented by some fine pieces from Worcester, Chelsea, Spode, Minton and

Wedgwood. The museum also has a copy of the famous Portland vase made in the Wedgwood factory.

The Salar Jung museum has some exquisite glass pieces drawn from Venice, France, Bohemia, America, Belgium, Istanbul and Czechoslovakia. It boasts some fine pieces of Persian and Indian glass. It also houses a large number of chandeliers, wall brackets, lamps and candelabras. Of particular interest are the coloured chandeliers which are a veritable feast for the eye.

The collection of clocks in the museum drawn from France, England, Switzerland, Germany, Holland and America include bird cage clocks, bracket clocks, grandfather clocks, and skeleton clocks. There are two outstanding clocks belonging to the period of Louis XIV of France. The clock which attracts the greatest number of visitors is a British bracket clock decorated with ormolu mounts in which a miniature toy figure strikes the gong at each hour.

Furniture

The European period furniture in the museum belongs to two main groups: French and English. There are four distinct styles in the French: Louis Quatorze (1643-1715), Louis Quinze (1715-1774), Louis Seize (1775-1793) and the Empire (pertaining to the Napoleonic period, 1804-1821). The special characteristic of the first (i.e. Louis XIV period) is Boulle work perfected by Andre Charles Boulle whose beautiful cabinets are part of the museum's collection.

During the period of Louis XV furniture making was elevated to an art, just like painting and sculpture. Rococo now extended to the field of furniture. The cabriole leg was in fashion and serpentine curves reigned supreme. The most celebrated piece in the museum is the exact replica of the 'Bureau du Roi', Louis XV's writing table. An important innovation of this period was the almirah with glass doors for use as a showcase.

Louis XVI's reign was marked by greater restraint and grace. The cabriole leg was supplanted by the straight leg. The museum has three suites of chairs belonging to this period.

Empire furniture, which is well represented in the museum, was marked by simplicity in design in decoration. Napoleon favoured the letter N in a Roman wreath and used ornaments of Roman design on his furniture. English furniture in the museum is represented by chairs designed by Robert Adam and Thomas Sheraton. There are also shield backed chairs in the style of George Hepplewhite, although it is not certain if these were actually designed by him.

The Salar Jung Library and Manuscript Collection

The museum's collection of art objects hogs the limelight; the library and manuscript collection have always been in the shadow. However, Salar Jung III's collection of books and manuscripts rivals his enormous collection of antiques and *objets d'art*. The library consists of 62,772 printed books of which 41,208 are in English, 13,027 in Urdu, 1,108 in Hindi, 1,105 in Telugu, 3,576 in Persian, 2,588 in Arabic and 160 in Turkish. There are 8,556 manuscripts in the museum. Among these, 2,623 are in Arabic, 4,815 in Persian, 1,096 in Urdu, and 22 in other languages. There are also 1,450 calligraphic panels in the collection. The English books include journals and albums of rare photos and engravings. The majority of English books were added by Salar Jung III. However, the collection of books which had been acquired by several preceding generations was given the form of a library by Sir Salar Jung I. The library also includes English translations of important works in Arabic, Persian, Sanskrit and Urdu. The oldest book in the collection is *The General History of the Turkes*... by Richard Knolles which was printed in AD1631. Since lack of space precludes a detailed discussion, it should suffice t say that the museum's manuscript collection is remarkable botl for its quality and quantity.

To preserve its rare books in digital form, the museum ha: entered into an agreement with the International Institute o1 Information Technology (IIIT), Hyderabad, for digitisation of books. The museum provides the facilities, and IIIT the manpower. IIIT has undertaken this work under the auspices of the Digital Library Project initiated by Carnegie Mellon University, Pittsburgh, USA. So far, more than 36,500 books have been scanned. The museum has also been associated with the National Mission for Manuscripts as a Manuscript Conservatior Centre since October 2003, for the conservation of manuscript: in Andhra Pradesh.

A Joy Forever

The statue of Salar Jung III stands outside solemnly facing the museum building. One wonders what the spry Nawab would have thought had he been alive. Would he have been happy at what posterity has done with his collection, or would he have felt let down? On the whole one thinks that he would have been pleased, even if his meticulousness for detail would have caused him to disapprove on certain occasions. It is for a responsive administration to be a faithful guardian of the priceless treasure-house of art that has been committed to its charge; and it is the duty of a responsible citizenry to ensure that the museum, described by Harendranath Chattopadhyaya as 'India's finest liberal university', is given the attention and care it deserves. Chattopadhyaya could not have put it any better when he wrote a poem called 'The Museum?' in March 1953, the first lines of which are:

This is no Museum – as it is said
For, as you know, a Museum is dead…
And this which millions shall come to see
Is all alive with immortality.

The poet also hit the nail on the head with the last lines of the same poem:

Prince of Collectors; you have come to stay
You are immortal and shall never pass away.

The Big Fat Hyderabadi Wedding

Dinaz Noria

The big fat Hyderabadi wedding has been getting bigger, more scrumptious, full of juice and topped with highly unusual, sometimes even bizarre events. To put this whole panoply of happenings together, it usually takes a lot of planning and effort.

Hyderabad is a happy mix of diverse communities most of whom take great pleasure in the business of marriage. There are large joint families which belong to even larger extended families.

In days gone by, it was the whole family that would come together to do the needful—teams would be formed, cousins would be given the responsibility of handling travel, arrivals, pick-ups, drops, etc., uncles would have to undertake the task of coordinating with the hotel or 'shaadi khana' as function halls used to be called, similarly relatives would be entrusted with the task of dealing with the caterers, entertainers, and designers... that is, us!

A typical Hyderabadi couple

In today's busy days, when precious few have the time to do anything but think of making more money than they ever thought, these duties are often entrusted to 'outsiders'. Professionals are called in to execute these duties. Wedding planners plan, designers design and decorate, caterers cater to food and drink requirements and so on. All the small details of the show are left to the experts. The planners look after most aspects of the wedding. They choreograph everything from inception, conception, execution and 'bankruption', all of it the whole canoodle! The invitation cards, venue and decor, the gifts, their packing and presentation, the food, clothes, with the possible exception of jewellery, are some of the aspects which are looked after by the planners. I recently read somewhere that thirty-three percent of the entire wedding budget is spent on jewellery alone, thirty percent on clothes, and mere mortals like us, the event stylists who beautify and decorate the event, have to be content with only three percent.

The *baarat* arrival into the city is treated with much fanfare. There are uniformed hostesses with welcome *aarti thaalis*, flowers and gifts to greet at arrival. Decorated cars and buses whisk them away to the hotel where another special welcome awaits them in the form of folk dancers, fire crackers and such *'dhoom dhaam'*. The revered *baaratis* are then escorted to their boudoirs which have welcome trays with yummy refreshments and snacks like suparis, *khaara*, chocolates, exotic fruit platters, cakes, etc. The rooms are decorated with flowers and scented candles. Each morning, they wake up to a crystal cup of *'chilla hua badam* soaked in *kesar'* accompanied with a poem on dawn; every night after the festivities are over the guests are bid sweet dreams with a silver glass of warm badaam milk. *Baaratis* are treated with kid gloves in most communities; they sometimes even have special areas demarcated for them at the wedding feast.

The *mehendi* and *sangeet* celebrations and the bachelor/bachelorette parties are the fun times of the wedding, unbridled by the more formal ceremonial functions. These used to be the domain of north Indians, but now have percolated down 'South' as well, endearing themselves to all people, community not withstanding. These functions involve much *'naach gaana'* together with fun and games. The families prepare skits to music—Bollywood rules closely followed by Tolly, Kolly and Polly...that for the uninitiated are colloquialisms for Telugu film industry, Kannada and Punjabi etc. Entertainment comes in the form of performances by stars, singers, djs, dancers, synchronised swimmers, fire eaters, and whatever the wallet can afford!

The *shaadi* however is a serious affair! Lots of rituals, many ceremonies, many rules to follow and to be broken or bent a wee bit these days. The auspicious *Saptpadi* or seven steps, seven promises to be kept, seven *pheras* around the fire or reading of holy verses for some, blessings with rice and flowers for others all culminate in one happy occasion—the wedding. It is followed by the reception and then the almost always tearful goodbye or the *bidai* ceremony, that's the cue for the curtains to be drawn. The bride and the groom jazz off for the honeymoon, guests go home, satiated, *baraatis* return laden with gifts, workers pull all the decorations down and planners? They sleep finally!

Hyderabad has a huge wedding industry. Venues that are very popular for weddings include the Ramoji film city where the entire wedding party can stay for the duration of the festivities. It offers a lot for innovation and ingenuous ideas to make the event special. The *sangeet* can be held on a railway platform with coolies as bearers, and food can be served on the railway tracks. Posters on the station can be custom made to depict the family, the bride and the groom. The wedding can take place in the ornate Mughal Garden which is no less grand than the *Jodha-Akbar* fantasy trip. Truly a full blown filmy affair!

The Taj Krishna is another popular venue, fabulously opulent with the distinction of being the most popular wedding address in town. It has a beautifully decorated hall coupled with a lush verdant lawn and adjacent gardens. Add the convenience of being located on the premier Road No 1 in Banjara Hills and the fact that it has 261 well-appointed rooms.

The Hyderabad International Convention Centre is fast growing in popularity as it has the distinct advantage of having a 60,500 sft of totally weather proof facility, that in a city which is known to have frequent April showers, a blistering summer, and an extended unreliable monsoon. It is a boon many have realised the importance of. Farwell to leaky shaky tarpaulin and cloth covered pandals.

Well aware of the Hyderabadi's love for good food, the city's top caterers vie with each other to invent newer ways to tease the palates of our connoisseurs. Tender almonds in a light gravy, dosas with corn and cheese and sprinklings of oregano and paprika, whole stuffed lamb roasted and so on. My favourite delicacy is Mahesh Sanghi's concoction of a whole alphonso mango which had its seed scooped out and filled with kesar kulfi. Indeed heaven on a plate!

Weddings in most communities are scheduled according to the auspicious dates. This results in long stretches of time which form the 'peak season' when there is hectic activity and brisk business and 'off-season' when there is plenty of free time for leisure. People connected with this industry usually just while away time waiting for work to start or have to find alternative means of gainful employment to tide over the fallow periods. When the season is on, there is hardly time to blink. For the people involved in the festivities, it is an endless rush of clothes, functions, jewellery, food, fun and frolic. Weddings in Hyderabad like the rest of the country are a time to get together and celebrate but what makes it special here is the fusion of old world charm with contemporary trends.

Art—a Way of Life

Fawad Tamkanat

I strongly believe that art is a way of life that frees the spirit revealing great truths hidden in the seemingly mundane. There is much veiled joy even in routine things, in monotony, and when daily events speak so loud, what need there is for one to have any message? The message is implicit in each and every thing we do, in each movement spent on doing it, and every space where it is done.

Simple subjects like the face of a woman, women shopping in bangle stores, Irani cafes, *haleem ki dukan*, labourers at Osman Gunj, street dogs and cows sitting at the roadside of Charminar, one of the most densely populated areas of Hyderabad, the dancing potrait of bonal, the Sufis at *dargah*, the *fakhirs* at shrines and the *sadhus* at temples can be perceived from multiple angles. All these images from the Hyderabad that I love and live in help me draw inspiration for my art. The thrill for me is in reaching their very essences.

Art was appreciated in my family in the form of literature. My father was a well-known Urdu poet Shaz Tamkanat. We are six brothers brought up in a very artistic environment. Poets, writers, musicians, and painters used to visit our home very often and we would sit with them in ghazal parties at home. Some of the important poets and musicians I met during my childhood are Kaifi Azmi, Javed Akhtar, Majrooh Sultan Puri, Begum Akhtar, Aziz Ahmed Khan Warsi, Syed Bin Mohd, Shabana Azmi and many more. I believe that my work has very strong influence of my father's poetry and his teaching about the concept of creativity.

As a painter, I have worked in various mediums like watercolour, dry point, etching, acrylic, and dry pastels on paper. I am now focusing on acrylic on canvas for my new series 'Street Observations'. Not so much photo-realistic and not quite figurative, it is very urban and sophisticated in style. A style that I believe typifies the new Hyderabad.

Here I would like to come back to my favourite subject—women. So far I have painted thousands of women especially portraying their face, voluptuous full body nudes besides hundreds of erotic drawings.

Faces of Women

Most of my painted women are tender and delicate; there is an element of innocence on their faces. There are young women who have not seen the harshness of life and they look so naïve. Then there are the faces I first saw in a women's college where I used to teach in the late 80s and early 90s during my post graduation. I left teaching decades ago, but the faces linger on my mind and my canvas even today. My women are young, urbanised and not yet in their 20s who like to dress up in colourful printed blouses, and decorate their foreheads with ornate *bindis* and eyes with *kaajal* and *surma*. They have aquiline noses and large doe-like eyes. My painted faces of young women at times resemble my friends whom I admire, and sometimes are a reflection of my fantasy of a perfect woman.

My woman's smile makes a man's heart skip a beat. There is anxiety in her eyes…the eyes ask: Will this man love me? Will he find me appealing? Will he take me home?

Female Nudes and Erotic Dry Points

In 1996 I was invited for the first time to an international installation camp 'Tide 96'. Here I got the opportunity to make erotic dry points in a printmaking studio. I worked with highly talented artists from all over the world during my three month stay in Europe. I was delighted to see the original masterpieces of Picasso, Van Gogh, Gauguin, Monet, Dega and many more. After I returned my work saw a transformation. For few years after that I focused mainly on black and white dry points, mostly erotic, and few large canvases of full body nudes of voluptuous women. One of my favourite work of that time was 'Harem of a Hyderabadi Nawab'.

For the past year and a half, I have been working on recreating the unique street culture of Hyderabad through my work and bringing it alive on my canvas. The streets of Hyderabad with its laidback air, the local people and their interesting quirks, and all those things that are so uniquely Hyderabadi, have captured my imagination since long. It's only now that I have been able to take time off to concentrate on this series, which has been on my mind always. And I must admit that this endeavour has brought me closer to my city, its people, its culture and above all, the essence of what makes one a Hyderabadi. Working on this series brought me out of my studio, onto the busy streets, the buzzing markets and before I knew, I was seeped into the rich culture of Hyderabad.

Of Naan and Irani *Chai*

On the way to my studio, I often used to observe the age-old Hyderabadi tradition of buying fresh naan from the tiny shops, for breakfast. People queue up in front of these cafes, early in the morning, and sip on Irani *chai*, while waiting for the naan to be prepared. This is a four hundred-year-old tradition of the city, and everything about it screams Hyderabadi—the method of cooking, the clothes of those who make the naan, the kind of crowd that gathers here—everything is a one-of-its-kind scenario. Talking of Irani *chai*, it is yet another important aspect of Hyderabad, truly unique to the people in this city. In the days of yore, Irani cafes were considered the hub of intellectuals. The scene has changed dramatically today, but it still is unique in every way possible. When I finally decided to transform these vivid images imprinted on my mind into paintings on the canvas, I stopped driving to the studio but started walking down the streets instead. I explored the lanes and by lanes of the city and clicked hundreds of pictures for hours together, capturing the mood of the city. Sometimes I carried my sketchbook and made drawings as and when something struck me.

When the city comes alive...

Ramzaan is the time to explore the Old City. And I decided to begin my adventure from Lad Bazaar. Glittering bangles, neon lights, bangle sellers who feel a woman's hand and decide what size of bangles she needs, and scores of burqa-clad women, jostling for space in the crowded stores—it is indeed a heady combo, a visual treat! I stood in these tiny, glittering stores, for hours on end, soaking in the festive feel and making sketches of the vivid scenes that played on before me. The haleem stores are another delight. Crowds throng to haleem stores in the Old

City in huge numbers to savour the city favourite, an authentic and mouth-watering delicacy. All this I tried to recreate on my canvas.

Folklore and fun fare

The Bonalu festival, a Hindu custom from the Telengana region of Andhra Pradesh, is another time of the year when the city comes alive with its vibrant cultural colours. Men who paint themselves like tigers, dance waving neem leaves, while women dressed like Goddess Kali, dance through the streets in a trance. It is a sight that has to be seen to be believed and I've given it its well-deserved place on my canvas.

Life stories

It's not always about customs and festivals alone. A city tells its story through its people too, and this I discovered when I noticed a young girl, who collected garbage on a rickshaw and sold scrap to fend for her family. Her grit tells an amazing story about the changing face of the girl child, who thrives despite all odds. I followed her to see what her day was like, and what I saw inspired me to immortalise her on my canvas.

The Mehboob of Hyderabad

Iqbal Patni

I safeguarded the eastern character of Hyderabad since its foundation. I am the stamp of Hyderabad. As an architectural monument synonymous with the city, with stately arches on the four sides, flanked by the grand Mecca Masjid and close proximity to the court of the Nizam at Punch Mohalla Palace, I symbolise the grandeur and past life...

I have witnessed the march of time for over four hundred years. If I am asked to pick one chapter from my voluminous memory bank that truly represented a glorious time then it will be the era of my beloved king Mehboob, the sixth Nizam of Hyderabad.

One may well ask: Why the saga of bygone years in today's modern times? I have keenly observed that it is always the influences from the past which become the inspirations for the future...

I am Charminar and the saga I narrate from the glorious past of Hyderabad commenced on 17 August 1866 with the birth of Mir Mehboob Ali Khan, who went on to become the sixth

Nizam of Hyderabad and whose deeds resonate across the city even today, if only one cares to hear...

Today happens to be the birthday of two-year-old Mehboob. On this special occasion the Dewans proceeded to the royal palace in a long procession of decorated elephants and armed guards to pay homage to the royal child. As royal etiquette forbade entry into the courtyard of the palace except on foot, they had to alight at the outer gate and stand respectfully with their faces turned towards the Mahal, from where the royal master was supposed to grace them. There they offered their royal *salaam* (right hand touching the ground as they bent low and then touching their forehead as they rose each time). The process was repeated at the entrance to the next courtyard till they arrived at a spot beyond which none were allowed to pass. Here they stood and wished the two-year-old prince on his birthday.

Young Mehboob received the best available modern education on one side and the influence of loyal and learned Nawab Salar Jung I on the other. The end result was that Hyderabad got the most charismatic and open-minded ruler to adorn the Asaf Jahi crown.

Mehboob acquired full control of the sovereign state of Hyderabad at a tender age. His first action as a ruler was to issue a royal proclamation to his subjects expressing his solitude with their happiness and welfare in the following words:

> Nothing will afford me greater pleasure than to see my people living in peace and prosperity, engaged in the development of their wealth, in the acquisition of knowledge and cultivation of arts and sciences, so that by their efforts the country may rise to a high state of enlightenment and the state derives support and benefit from their knowledge and intelligence.

It is my earnest hope that the ministers and all the officers of the state relying on my protection and support, will always be zealous in promotion of good and suppression of evil and shall protect the rights of the people without, fear or favour.

Thus began *Mehboob ka Daur* earnestly on its dazzling course. It was destined to be an era of unprecedented tranquility and amazing contradictions. Gone were the days of the state's uncertain finances and indifferent administration. Schools, colleges, libraries, reading rooms, public gardens, railways, electricity, hospitals, telegraph and telephone services were introduced during Mehboob's era, which truly heralded the rise of the educated urban middle class that forms the backbone of any society even today.

Judicial system came into being; civil and criminal courts were established in all subas of the state; legal profession became organised; jurisprudence and case laws began to receive proper attention. Thus justice became accessible to even the common people. Almost every department that was the part of the British administration was set up in Hyderabad and worked with creditable efficiency.

In absolute monarchies of that time, people's rights, public-spirited administration and ruler's accountability were just far fetched ideas. However, Mehboob's humane and conscientious nature resulted in an administration that was not only competent but also fair minded and devoid of any religious intolerance. Thus, the personality of a ruler has a marked influence upon the conditions of life in his state; it lends a style and colour to his surroundings, and dominates even those changes which time gradually brings about.

The sense of charity and understanding was part of Mehboob's persona. His personal munificence was legendary. This persona of the sovereign percolated down the pyramid of hierarchy and brought about times of amazing individual generousity. Those who were in a position to help the less fortunate did so ungrudgingly without hurting the recipients of self-esteem.

The house of Nizam under Mehboob reconciled itself to the reality that power was indeed paramount in theory and without proper delegation can never result in peace and prosperity of the people. Thus the first ever legislative council was created in the State of Hyderabad. With the establishment of the council, the business of governance was taken out of the inaccessible palace and/or the dewan's exclusive chambers to a large extent.

Further steps were taken by Mehboob in this direction through a comprehensive document in which he analysed with deep insight the deficiencies of past systems, highlighting the present day need and spelling out the tasks ahead for future. He declared in this document that the character of a government could only be judged by the extent of its contributions to not only public peace and prosperity but also to solvency of its exchequer.

Mehboob delegated part of his powers to the council. Such voluntary delegation by a monarch was unheard of at that time and by doing so he exhibited a sense of understanding of the changing times. His led his whole life in grandeur without ostentation and in dignity without assumption of state. But such grandeur and dignity only set off the inborn simplicity of his nature. No wonder people felt awed in his presence.

The story of Mehboob will not be complete without a few anecdotes attached to his personal life, but we are here to take those larger lessons from his short lifespan of forty-five years which loom in front of us in the form of true secularism, progressive actions and governance that aimed at benefiting the common man. The concern and care for the people of Hyderabad shown by Mehboob as absolute monarch of this sovereign state who was above question and accountability is without parallel even today, when the Constitution of India holds its elected rulers fully accountable for their actions.

That Hyderabad, alas, no longer exists except in the hearts of those who survived it.

Ganga-Jamuna Culture

Lakshmi Devi Raj

Those were the days when Hyderabad was a different city with a distinct culture of its own—a unique Ganga-Jamuna culture. We never identified ourselves as Hindus or Muslims but only as Hyderabadis! I grew up knowing people as so and so *chacha* and so and so aunt, never as a Hindu or a Muslim.

My childhood in Hyderabad was very beautiful—so different from what I see today. We went to school, came home and then played with my sister and cousins—yes, it was a large joint family consisting of my grandmother, a beautiful old lady, my father's brothers and their families. I remember my fair grandmother, a widow in a white saree with head covered—she used to tell us such interesting mythological stories and moral tales. The *Karthik Maas* (beginning of winter) especially was a very exciting time for us children. There were no geysers so water was heated in a *bhupka*. The servants would rise up early, heat the water and carry buckets of hot water to all the senior ladies of the house who would finish their puja before sunrise. We children were all ready by dawn and would sit around our grandma near an

Amla tree, where she would finish the puja and then tell us a moral story. We used to greedily eye the dry fruit laddoos on the silver tray—each one of us got one every day for a whole month during *Karthik Maas*.

Every Sunday, washing my hair was a long and leisurely ritual. The *ayah* would oil my hair after breakfast, then wash it after a couple of hours. Coal fire in earthenware was placed on a *takhat* and *agar barmaki* was put in the fire, which was then covered with a woven basket. I would lie down and she would spread my hair over the basket. The hair would dry gradually and the fragrance would last till the next hair wash! At 8.00 am our Urdu master sahib or tutor would arrive punctually to teach us Urdu. Our own Dakhni language was an amalgamation of Telugu, Persian and Hindi with a flavour of Marathi and Kannada. The

Drying hair the old fashioned way

Hyderabad state then comprised of Telangana, Marathwada and Karnataka. I had learnt a little Marathi from the *pujaris* who came home everyday for *puja*. My uncles and munshi sahib Ranga Rao taught me a little Telugu also. Everyday we went to school in a beige colored Baby Ford car. Yes, this car was called *bachchon ki gadi* (children's car). It had light sea green silk purdah (curtains) for the ladies of the house to use if they went to the old city to visit our relatives.

I must talk about my beloved school Mehbubia—the cars pulled up at a door that led to the main school area—the *purdah* gate—and two *ayahs* held up a curtain from the car to the door! There were not more than twenty girls in a class. Family background was important and admission was strict. It was as good as any international finishing school. Hindu or Muslim— we used to celebrate all festivals together. My friends would come home to play Holi, enjoy watching our servants playing *bathkamma* and stay back for dinner. It was a must for them to come to my place for lunch on Dussera and Diwali and I looked forward to my lunches during Id-ul-Fitr and Bakrid.

I remember attending weddings decked up in rich clothes and jewellery as a girl. My mother had a woman servant to carry her *paandaan* with her wherever she went. The weddings were celebrated at home with family, relatives and friends. The whole town was not invited as is the precedence now. My sister and I would go with my mother into the Zenana (female) section of the house where the rooms would have farsh (white sheets) sprinkled with mica, beautiful carpets along the walls with *gao takias* and a *paandaan* and *ugaldaan*. Dinner was served on the floor, no buffets. In Hindu weddings, food was served on banana leaves or *patroli* wth clay *katoris* and a wooden platter to sit on. For a Muslim wedding, a red *dastarkhaan* would be spread and food laid on it. People sat around the *dastarkhaan* or on *chowkis* and ate. There would be *qawwalis* or nautch girls to entertain the guests.

The parties of those days were fun and yet not noisy. Music was not played so loudly as it is done today; people rather enjoyed listening to ghazal singers or qawwals. I remember when Begum Akhtar sang every night for a whole month at Prince Mozam Jah's after dinner till the wee hours! It was simply fantastic! In 1954 when I was entertaining Mrs Jackie Kennedy Onasis, Aziz Ahmed Khan Warsi sang after dinner for a couple of hours, and Jackie enjoyed the rhythm and the beat of the music while I was explaining the verses.

After Mehbubia, I joined the OU Women's College where Miss Hivell was our principal. Before her Begum Jain Y. J. was the principal who was a scholar in Sanskrit. Women in the late nineteenth and twentieth century were well educated. Mrs Zeenat Sajida is an institution by herself while Mrs Rafia Sultana was a Reader in Urdu at the University. The women's college staff constituted of only ladies, who were highly qualified. After finishing my graduation, I wanted to take up a job but my mother was dead against it. My father had tried to teach driving to my older cousins who never got round to learn it. I was the first in my class to learn driving. I started it in the first year of my college in 1951. Mrs Tehmenabai Dhage and Mrs Arjunanand Wahabudding used to drive and I was inspired seeing them. I wanted to be able to drive like them. I remember I had once gone to Maj. Gur to ask for an appointment, and he just lifted his telephone and called up my mother saying, 'Rani sahib, I'm sending her back home. Don't allow her to go about like this.' Once I went to uncle Shiv K. Lal to tell him about traffic conditions; he did the same. It showed their concern and made me realise the respect they had for my family.

I joined the OU University for a diploma course in French during 1963-64. I used to leave my house at 8.45 am to be in the University by 9.00 am. I literally used to drive like a mad woman, trying to fly, not drive. My mother always got worried and gave me a lecture on safety, asking me to leave ten minutes early instead of racing to college. I always used to criticise uncle Fijazuddin Sahib, chief architect, for the way Raj Bhavan was planned. He got special admission for me at the Vanita exit grounds for classes in architecture. To go back to college after a gap of almost five years was rather harrowing. I tried, but my weak maths (2 and 2 never made 4 for me—I was and still am bad at calculations!) prevented me from mastering the subject. I even got a tutor at home to teach me maths. He threw a bombshell by uttering the word theorem (I had never heard of it before!). So I could never become an architect. It was Mr Fiyaz's greatness and kindness to have supported me in this endeavour. They were all such gracious and loving people. I can also never forget Uncle L.N. Gupta (IAS) for as long as I live.

Till about 1948, we would go away in summer to either Ooty or Kashmir and return a day before the school re-opened. If my father was out of the country with H.H. Princess D, then we would go to our farmhouse in Vicarabad, which was ten degrees cooler than Hyderabad. Even there the holidays were exciting. There was no electricity. Only gas lamps were used and water was pumped out of the well with the help of two oxen. We children would drive up to the railway station to fetch ice, fresh fruits and vegetables, and the best part was the ice-cream soda in large glasses with ice in them! Vicarabad had delicious mangoes, chikoos, fresh eggs and chicken. The house had tamarind and neem trees all around the farm. My father's elder brother would have a small room constructed with *thatis* and *khus* curtains and would teach Urdu to the poor children. The whole house had *khus* curtains, which were watered every few hours, and the rooms were cool in the afternoons. Ceiling fans with cloth and frill had a rope attached; the servants' children used to love to sit and gently wave the fans since it was so cool and shaded in there!

I still cherish my summer trip to Ooty once when H.H and princess M were also there in Snowdon House. We used to play hide and seek and other games. Princess M would always take my sister as partner because she was slim like her and poor me was made to run. We also spent a glorious holiday in Gulmarg where H.H. P.D and P.N joined us in the evening to play tug-of-war. What fun we had! Do today's children have such a carefree childhood?

It is a different Hyderabad now! Developed but at what cost? Is this town planning, buildings, apartments, commercial and residential complexes mushrooming haphazardly where they please with no regard for heritage and architecture that needs to be preserved? These are important questions for each Hyderabadi that need to be addressed. I wish the old Hyderabad was left untouched and the development had taken place in the periphery of the city. Yes, we do need change, but change for the better should be welcome.

Another Day, Another Time

Mithi Chinoy

As I walk through the streets of Hyderabad,
I recall the greatness and glory of fellow Parsis of the Nizam era
who brought the community stability and prosperity.

I am forty-five today and from a Hyderabad, rich with the legacy of rulers, kingdoms, opulence, majesty, gracious living and men of vision. But today's Hyderabad of which I am an intrinsic part is modern, a global IT hub and a cosmopolitan city of the world.

So much has changed since my childhood that I think it's time I take a walk around this beautiful city and recollect its history, legendary experiences and beautiful times that are hidden behind Hyderabad's old buildings and beautiful bungalows, in its streets and monuments and most of all in people's memories.

Here I am on Naya Pul, walking amid rickshaw pullers, cyclists, pedestrians and motorists. Walking is difficult here due to the burgeoning traffic but I am fortunate to quickly leave it behind me and, after a short walk, find myself facing the majestic Salar Jung Museum, comprising a collection of artefacts, *objet d'art* and jewels of Salar Jung III.

Chaos and Confusion

Standing before it, I am reminded of the stories narrated to me by my family about the legendary Sir Salar Jung I, and of life in Hyderabad in 1853. This was the time when the state was in utter 'chaos and confusion' and heavy arrears, says my septuagenarian aunt, Dr Polly Chenoy. Besides, the British government had made some huge claims on the Nizam, amounting to rupees forty-five lakhs.

The bankruptcy of the Hyderabad government forced the administration in a complete disarray, while the non-payment of the British troops was seen as a grave political evil. To remedy the situation, a treaty was signed between the British and the then Nizam in 1853 under which the British maintained the existing Hyderabad contingent force in lieu of the troops that the Nizam was to furnish on demand during war time.

That was when Sir Salar Jung I, Nawab Mukhtar-ul-Mulk, Hyderabad state's most dynamic Prime Minister, stepped in to restore financial stability and a sound administration. He did this by inviting honest, able, and loyal professionals from different parts of India. These were the Parsis, who came from Jalna, Maharashtra. Sir Salar Jung I was convinced that these English-speaking men would contribute their great insight and dedication to offices in general administration, customs, revenue, the postal department, the judiciary, mint, medicine, and as translators to the Paigahs or aristocratic landlords under the Nizam.

The fact that the Parsis were fluent in English was a big asset; not only could they act as intermediaries between outsiders to the state and the natives but also skilfully execute the job entrusted to them. They knew Persian too, which helped them with the administration of the state and in following the customs and traditions laid down here. No wonder, then, the Parsis were highly regarded by the powers that be in Hyderabad dominions.

Entrepreneurial Skills

Apart from these men who joined the Nizam's service, there were many other Parsi entrepreneurs who dealt with China and later settled here in Hyderabad. They came here, deep into the cotton heartland to exploit the business potential of exporting cotton from the Deccan to newly established mills in Mumbai. They also set up ginning and spinning factories in Adilabad, Jalna, Berar, Gulbarga and Bhainsa.

In fact, Shapurji Edulji Chenai, who was in the service of the Paigah Nawab, Rashiduddin Khan, was given a lakh of rupees for safe keeping by his employer. Two years later, when the Paigah Nawab asked for his money back, he was pleasantly surprised to find it doubled! Shapurji explained that he had invested in cotton and foodgrains and also loaned money at high rates of interest.

The Nawab refused to take his money back, and scolded Shapurji for loaning a Muslim's money on interest. So, Shapurji used the money to trade in cotton and in the early 1880s, he set up his own cotton mills in Gulbarga, Hyderabad State, called the Mahboobshahi Mills.

As I come out of my recollection of days gone by, I gaze fondly at the museum and my environs, the Musi River flanked by the Osmania General Hospital and the High Court and in the far distance, the Chowmohalla Palace.

Pestonshahi Sikka

The government of Hyderabad state was in safe hands, with the Parsis in important advisory and administrative positions. But that was not all. Industry and integrity were a healthy combination in the two brothers, Viccaji and Pestonji Meherji. These two brothers, of humble origins, were successful bankers and jagirdars to the Nizam. They helped the Nizam's government with timely financial support and in return, were granted the right to collect taxes in Berar.

In time, Pestonji Meherji was appointed as Bakshi or Paymaster of the Hyderabad contingent in lieu of which he was granted the right to strike coins in the Marathwada region. For the first time, the brothers were permitted to have their own initials and marks engraved on national coins. In 1840, they minted their own silver coins, called the 'Pestonshahi Sikka' which bore their initials.

The Meherji brothers are best remembered for their various charitable activities, including building the first Dar-e-Meher (Fire Temple) in Secunderabad, and four others, four Dokhmas (Towers of Silence) at Sholapur, Belapur, Aurangabad and Hyderabad, besides schools and other institutions. The Dar-e-Meher built by the Meherji brothers is called the Junni Agiari (Old Fire Temple). It is now known as the Viccaji-Meherji Agiari and is adjacent to the Cherma's store on busy M.G. Road.

Secunderabad, a City of Prosperity

Remembrances of my hometown Secunderabad and sister city to Hyderabad take me there and I'm happy to be in familiar surroundings. Secunderabad is important to the history of the Parsis of the twin cities because here's where the majority of them settled down even when it was growing from strength to strength as a Cantonment town. Since the army enjoyed certain concessions under the Subsidiary Alliance, bankers (shroffs) and merchants were drawn to Secunderabad, Hyderabad's twin city.

This was where my forefathers and other Parsis settled down and prospered. They flourished under the Nizam, excelled under his patronage and were recognised with impressive and high-sounding titles on important days. My aunt Goolbanoo Y. Chenoy, present President of the Parsi Zoroastrian Anjuman of Hyderabad and Secunderabad (PZASH), recalls the glittering durbar ceremonies hosted by the Nizam in which he granted titles and lands for excellence in various streams of life. She recalls the pomp with which the Nizam H. E. H. Mir Osman Ali Khan conferred on her uncle the title of Nawab Erach Yar Jung Bahadur, Agent-General of Berar, one of the highest offices of the land.

But he was not alone in his ascent to fame and glory, there were others too. They were Nawab Sir Faridoon-ul-Mulk Bahadur, President of the Executive Council of the Nizam; Nawab Barzo Jung Bahadur, Commissioner of Revenue; Nawab Sohrab Nawaz Jung and Nawab Rustom Jung, both Commissioners of Customs, and Rustomji Jamshedji Chenoy, Postmaster General. The Home Secretary's post was given to Hormusji Vakeel; Pestonji Bapooji Chenoy was made Mint Master and had the rare distinction of being the first Indian to hold that post.

Nawab Darab Jung Bahadur was made the Sadr-ul-Moham of the Sarf-e-Khas Mubarak, while Faridoon S. Chenoy was made Chief Engineer of Hyderabad State, Dr Coorlawala, Chief Medical Officer to the Nizam was titled Nawab Rustom Yar Jung Bahadur and C.B. Taraporewala was Financial Adviser of H.E.H the Nizam Mir Osman Ali Khan Bahadur, Asaf Jah VII. Another important achiever was Barrister Noshir Chenoy, the only Parsi barrister in the twin cities and a legal luminary.

The efforts of Faridoonji Vaccha can never go unrecognised in the annals of the time as he was responsible for Revenue and Settlement works in Aurangabad. For his good work in the area, the Nizam H.E.H. Mehboob Ali Pasha gifted him a gold watch and chain, but that was just the beginning. He later rose to eminence to win titles such as Taluqdar of Aurangabad, followed by Commissioner of Hyderabad and Private Secretary to Sir Salar Jung II.

In later years, he was variously titled: Sadr-ul-Maham Ekhtassasi (Extraordinary member without a portfolio), Nawab Faridoon Jung Bahadur, Faridoon-ud-Daula Bahadur and Faridoon-ul-Mulk Bahadur. The British also decorated him with the C.I.E. (1903), C.S.I. (1911), K.S.I.E. (1913) and C.B.E. (1918).

Religious and Social Bodies

Even as tales of my forefathers and other members of my community flash before my eyes, I come back to reality, only to face landmarks and Parsi monuments with which I have had a long association. As I walk down from Paradise junction, I can see the two Dar-e-Mehers and the Parsi Dharamsala, the latter a venue for many beautiful weddings and navjotes even today. Behind me, on S.P. Road stands the Zoroastrian Club, a sports and social venue for the community.

Across the street from the Viccaji-Meherji Agiari, the Parsi Zoroastrian Anjuman of Hyderabad and Secunderabad (PZASH), the governing body of the community, built another Fire Temple or Dar-e-Meher, which is fondly called Navi Agiari or 'New Fire Temple.' This temple was built on the munificence of Shapoorji Edulji Chenai, Private Secretary to Nawab Sir Khursheed Jah Bahadur, and Parsi donors. It was later called the Seth Khanbahadur Edulji Chenai Anjuman Dar-e-Meher. Later, a Dokhma was also built.

In about 1904, the Bai Maneckbai Nusserwanji Chenoy Fire Temple was built at Tilak Road, Abids, with money from Maneckbai Chinoy, once she realised how difficult it was for people to go to the Fire Temples in Secunderabad. People would have to travel by bullock carts and horse-driven tongas to reach the temple in Secunderabad. The Dar-e-Meher is a simple brick-and-lime mortar structure built in European architectural style of architecture, and is perhaps largely influenced by the nineteenth century British administered Residency Bazaar, whose architectural style was chiefly European.

Once the temple was built, Parsi philanthropists donated generously for the construction of residential blocks in the temple compound. As a result, thirty-seven families live in these blocks. Full time priests are provided with separate quarters. In addition, there is a marriage and religious hall, an office and a hall for revaan bangle (funeral ceremonies).

When the PZASH was being established, it was the eminent lawyer Nadirshah Bapooji Chenoy, brother of Nawab Darab Jung Bahadur, who helped largely with the drafting of its Trust Deed to make it viable with the provisions of the Indian Constitution. He later also assisted in making the Seth Khanbahadur Edulji Chenai Anjuman Dar-e-Meher the main religious institution of this Deed, and later confirmed it as a religious Trust. He was a scholar of Persian and Zoroastrian history, and co-founder of the Hyderabad Industrial Trust Fund with Mir Laik Ali and Gulam Mohammed, who later became President of Pakistan.

Turning into Park Lane, I see the Bai Ratanbai J. Chenoy Charitable Dispensary which has provided medical help to many and the neighboring Bai Ratanbai Jehangarji Chinoy Parsi High School, which is one of the city's finest schools. Students excel in academics and sports and bring pride to their alma mater.

Adjacent to the Bai Ratanbai Jehangarji Chinoy Parsi High School was a large estate, better known as 116-118 Park Lane.

My forefathers lived on this estate and established a shop there called the Europe Shop, which sold all kinds of Chinese artefacts, giving them the sobriquet of 'Chinaiwalla' or dealers in Chinese ware. Around the shop were large mansions and on the main road was the beautiful marble mansion of Sohrab Nawaz Jung called Sohrab Manzil.

Other stately mansions with beautifully laid out gardens and large estates were the large estates of Nawab Erach Yar Jung at Tarbund, Shapoorwadi at Hill Fort, Hyderabad and Chinoy Mansion at P.G. Road, Secunderabad. In fact, the present day Taj Mahal Hotel, Abid Road, belonged to the family of the Nakras and was a symbol of gracious living. Another stately home was that of Nawab Rustom Yar Jung Bahadur, known as 'Craigmoore'. It was heavily influenced by European architecture and was opposite the Secretariat building.

As time went by and the Parsis prospered, they began to own property in different parts of Secunderabad beginning with Marredpally and going all the way to present-day Prenderghast Road, Tarbund, Bowenpally and Trimulgherry. In fact, in time they also owned one side of the street of present-day Park Lane.

Other old and established families who came into their own at the time were the Italias, Rustomframs, Barias and Parakhs. Of them, D.D. Italia became a member of the Rajya Sabha in the 1950s, and four generations later, his great grandson, Lord Karan Bilimoria, CBE, DL, is better known as an entrepreneur, founder and chief executive of Cobra Beer, UK. Born and educated in Hyderabad, Karan is the pride of fellow Parsis here.

Great Foresight

In their own advancement, the community did not forget the less fortunate among them. They constructed housing colonies for the poor in Bapu Bagh, Shapur Bagh and around the three Dar-e-Mehers of the twin cities. In the late 1950s, the Zoroastrian Stree Mandal was formed as a ladies chapter by Soona J. Chinoy as a social service organisation. It continues to do good work even today.

Life and Times

Due to the close proximity to the Nizam's court, the Parsis of the twin cities adapted to the local lifestyle. While some women maintained partial purdah by curtaining their car windows, others embellished their clothes with zardozi and wore typical Hyderabadi jewellery like the famous *satlada* (seven rows of pearl necklaces, starting from shortest and moving progressively to the longest row), Basra pearls and intricately patterned jewellery inlaid with gemstones.

Satlada Necklace

Often, Parsi children of aristocratic families were taken to court to present a nazrana (gift) of a gold ashrafi (coin) to the Nizam. At school, they learnt Persian, Urdu and Telugu, and at home Gujarati. The elders patronised shairi and qawwali and read Persian literature.

Hospitality

The Parsis were traditional in their outlook and God-fearing, and generous and thoughtful to the less fortunate. In the larger and established homes, food was cooked for about twenty-five to thirty people per day, and those who came to Secunderabad from out of town and stayed at the Dharamsala were invited to dine with them.

The Parsis of Hyderabad and Secunderabad entertained in lavish style. Their large and beautiful all-marble homes were the venues of the most delightful dinners. Parties were frequent, and had the cream of society attending. They were formal parties, heavily influenced by both the local aristocracy and the British in terms of cuisine and service. Dinners hosted by Nawab Erach Yar Jung and his wife Begum Tehmina Yar Jung were by far the loveliest in town as they entertained in the most lavish style.

Women loved to attend coffee mornings, which always began punctually at 11 am. Bridge, rummy and mah-jong were games women enjoyed playing regularly through the week, as they do even now. If youngsters longed to go to Hilla Chinoy's badminton parties at Chinoy Mansion, the older ladies enjoyed visiting each other.

Weddings were a treat for sore eyes. Everyone longed to see which sari and jewellery Soona J. Chinoy wore, or Roshanbanoo Coorlawala or even Khorshed Bahman Surti. Heads often turned to see Homai C. Taraporewala and Jerbanoo N. Chenoy's jewellery and matching saris as they walked in to weddings and navjotes at the Parsi Dharamsala. Women in garas of classic colours—red, orange, maroon, black and purple—kors or embroidered sari borders in delicate floral style embroidered by Sheroo Munshi swished by until the evening drew to a close. It was a pageant of the most gorgeous sari and jewellery collection.

The affluent Parsis drove around in foreign cars—Hoshang Chinoy drove a black Cadillac, while Nawab Erach Yar Jung owned a classy wine-coloured Cadillac, Dara Shahpurji Chenai drove a Rolls Royce while Dr Bahman Surti drove a Ford. Captain Kayarman Pestonji is the proud owner of a range of vintage cars that he displays from time to time.

Since the fall of the Nizam's rule and the formation of Andhra Pradesh in 1956, the Parsi community in Hyderabad and Secunderabad have made progress in leaps and bounds. The young have taken up competitive professions and are very successful too.

And true to our promise to King Jadhav Rana of Sanjan 1300 years ago, the Parsis of the twin cities continue to sweeten the land with their good thoughts, words and deeds, a teaching of the prophet Zoroaster.

This article is based on facts provided by kind courtesy of Dr Polly N. Chenoy, author of *Contribution of the Parsis to the Administration of the Nizams of Hyderabad.*

A Precious Legacy called Theatre

Mohammad Ali Baig

Circa 1984: Sunday, 3 June. Hyderabad woke up to the shocking news of the rather untimely demise of Qadir Ali Baig sahib at an age of forty-six. 'End of an era' screamed a headline in the leading English daily. Other publications, especially Urdu vernaculars, had their supplements filled with obituaries and tributes for him for the rest of the week.

Circa 2004: It was after almost a decade that I was relocating to Hyderabad, thanks to my ad films assignments taking me to seven cities across five countries, keeping me away from home, and my favourite city. This homecoming turned more eventful since it coincided with the twentieth anniversary of Baba's (dad's) passing away. It was an occasion that Hyderabad's theatre, literary and arts fraternity were commemorating along with the Information & Broadcasting Ministry. The occasion was momentous, the atmosphere emotion-charged. Twenty years later, friends and admirers, fans and peers gathered on a chilly Sunday morning in 2004 to remember and pay their tributes to an artist who was not just a towering theatre legend but also a gem of a human being. When they spoke about him in choked voices with tear-filled eyes, it didn't seem like they were paying their tribute to one of India's most accomplished theatre artists after two decades, but as if they were talking about someone who had left us just the previous day. On that occasion, it was decided and declared that a foundation shall be set up in his name as a fitting tribute; a platform to revive theatre in Hyderabad and bring it back to the days when Baba was alive, with the quality and frequency of productions that marked the 1970s and early 1980s as the 'golden era' of Hindustani theatre in Hyderabad. As theatre and cinema veteran Shri M.S.Sathyu said, 'When theatre in Hyderabad was bogged down in cliches both in form and content, the Qadir Ali Baig wave made history in Hyderabad. He gave theatre a new direction but the cruel hands of death snatched him away from us forever in the midst of his young, fruitful years. It is in the fitness of things that a Foundation be set up in his name'. So, the Qadir Ali Baig Theatre Foundation came into being and began its journey. And with it started my second-coming into theatre. Before I knew it, a committee chaired by my mother Begum Razia Baig, who had in her calm and graceful way lent unrelenting support to Baba's legendary theatre movement, was formed comprising some of the country's most respected luminaries from theatre, cinema and related arts. And the mantle of spearheading the revival movement fell on my rather weak shoulders.

Circa 2008: So, here we are today with a revived theatre scene in Hyderabad, rejuvenated with about two dozen quality theatre evenings in just a little over two years with almost the entire top end of the country's theatre professionals like Naseeruddin Shah, Shabana Azmi, Habib Tanvir, M.S.Sathyu, Rohini Hattangady, Amal Allana, Nadira Babbar, Ram Gopal Bajaj, Jabbar Patel, Arundhati Nag, the National School of Drama, IPTA and others, a growing audience base that is buying even a thousand rupee ticket to watch good theatre, media that is supportive more than ever and corporate sponsorship that is coming by encouragingly. As importantly, this moment of reckoning is also serving as a shot-in-the-arm for local amateur theatre groups who are accelerating their efforts with renewed vigour, and some others who have started re-grouping.

In retrospect, I wouldn't have treaded on this tough path if it was not as a tribute to Baba or for the city of Hyderabad, right in that order! Though I had spent spans of time in various cities, Bangalore in particular longer than any other, travelled as part of my elder brother Moin Ali Baig's entourage and a producer to prestigious, high-brow theatre festivals in the US and in India, had friends from the field in places like Israel, eastern Europe, South Africa and far East, never did any city compel me to return to theatre like this glorious city of Hyderabad. There's something in the air here that leaves you inspired and committed more than any place else. Perhaps the inspiration comes from majestic edifices like the impregnable Golconda Fort, the largest fortress in ruins in the world. Or the imposing Charminar, that is still the face of the city about four-and-a-half centuries after it was constructed. The *ganga-jamuni tehzeeb*, the inimitable way of life that taught us to be Hyderabadis first, Muslims, Hindus, Parsis, Christians, Jews or Sikhs later. That showed us that *Hyderabadiyat* was, and still is, a sense of patriotism. Or perhaps from the Qutub Shahs, the founders of this city, who not just preached but also practised arts and true cosmopolitanism over four centuries ago, turning the citadel of their power into an active practising centre of arts and culture. It was they who gave the first Urdu *sahib-e-diwan* to the country, and as commendably had the vision to dream big for their city and the courage and conviction to execute it. While they left eternal impressions on the city's culture and landscape, Asaf Jahs, popularly known as the Nizams and progressive

Hyderabad's architects post Mughal-invasion of the Deccan, shaped our lifestyle mingling sensuously the Mughal, Dakhni (Deccani), Persian, and European influences in rituals, cuisine, costumes and language. We certainly don't realise today that Hyderabad owes a lot to these two dynasties.

The late Qadir Ali Baig sahib's theatre evolved from this cyclorama of history and cultural heritage. His themes were always socially relevant and message oriented, mounted with epic visual imagery and production set-ups. As thespian Shri Habib Tanvir observed, 'It can't be a mere coincidence that Qadir Ali Baig lived for forty six years and did forty six plays. It is sheer destiny, he was born to do so. He had a natural flair for dialogue writing and if he had more years to live he would have done wonders'. Trendsetting historical pageants like 'Quli Qutub Shah' at the precinct of Rani Mahal at the Golconda Fort, 'Mahboob' at the Aiwan-e-Aali of the Chowmoholla Palace inspired many other directors to produce plays at heritage locations in other cities. Theatre could not have been any less spectacular for someone born with more than the proverbial bejewelled silver spoon, trained initially to take over his father's mantle of championing polo, breeding and racing the sub-continent's finest derby winners. A youngster whose birthday gifts included a convertible sports Jaguar and Bentleys by a father whose conquests on polo fields were as legendary as his lifestyle in those days, what with a two-seater jet at his disposal to take him to various polo playing centres across Europe along with HRH the Prince of Berar. Still, when he travelled to perform socially meaningful theatre across the country, in the later part of his life, with his repertory, the New Theatre of Hyderabad, he travelled second-class with the rest of the crew. That was his level of commitment to the art form and he would be remembered as someone who always led by example. To quote eminent Kannada playwright and director Prasanna: 'Hailing from the most upper crest of society, Qadir saab disrobed himself of his elitist attire to devote his life to theatre. Hallmark of a true artist.' In one of his interviews to the press, sadly in what turned out to be his last one, answering a question about what theatre means to him Baba had said, 'For me every rehearsal is like pooja and each show Eid'. That was what theatre meant to him—Devotion and Celebration! Today when we perform, we celebrate. We celebrate theatre in his memory.

As in the words of former director and acting Chairman of the National School of Drama, Shri Mohan Maharishi, 'Post-independence Indian theatre has seen stalwarts like Prithviraj Kapoor in Mumbai, Ebrahim Alkazi in Delhi, Shambhu Mitra in Kolkata and Qadir Ali Baig in Hyderabad'. His was and always will be a larger-than-life-persona for Hyderabad. As a child I always imitated him—the way he dressed, the style of his lighting a cigar, his way of mounting a horse, even trying the fragrance of his favourite cologne. As a professional, I always try to emulate him. He was exemplary in blending art and commerce in his work, a task most of us find very difficult to achieve—a unique blend that I try to get in my work. While his plays received critical acclaim, they were equally enjoyed by the masses. His devotion to theatre and its unprecedented success in the Deccan, however, was never at the cost of our family life, a kind of curse that all we professionals can do without these days. A perfectionist and a keen observer of the minutest detail, he would spend months on scripts, characters, cast, sets, costumes meticulously, never forgetting to pick up the most suitable birthday gift for any of us. It is inspiring to have seen a legendary figure taking the little trouble to make the simplest ceremony at home all the more special whether for my mom, either of my two siblings or even for the large domestic staff. My work both in ad films and theatre is modelled on his creations. When I had set out to make the country's biggest ad film, though without realising it, it was this inspiration that enabled me to lead a 250-member crew from six countries delivering a memorable job. Though the experience of some of them in Hollywood equalled my age!

The million dollar epic ad film is a case study in production management and post production today. The overwhelming audience response and national media acclaim to Foundation's theatre productions like 'Taramati-The Legend of An Artist' at the two-hundred year old Taramati Baradari monument, 'His Exalted Highness' at the Khilwat mubarak of Chowmahalla Palace and 'Raat Phoolon Ki', an unique production of interpretation of poetry with theatre, dance and live music are wavering steps, attempts in the direction of revisiting his work. In the process, I revisit my childhood, while Hyderabad revisits its heritage, and accepts theatre as a way of life. As you may see for yourself, theatre is not just an art form or a passion for me, it is an invaluable legacy. When two generations and five members of your family have served it, it can't be anything less precious.

The personal side of a Legend

Despite all his pre-occupation with horses at the stud farm, polo and races in the early part of his life and theatre later, Baba always made my birthdays special and unforgettable. It was of significance that on each of the day the three of us were born, we had our stud farm horses win classic derbies. As a child, I thought that those gold cups that would be brought home from the races in the evening was our birthday present. And I grew up looking forward to such a gift every birthday. What I ended up getting on one of those was far more valuable. It was my last birthday with Baba on 15 January 1984, the year that Baba passed away, and I was just about getting into my teens. He was ailing from his fatal renal problem and birthday celebration was the last thing on any of our minds. But early that morning I saw him walking into my room to give me the daily papa bear hug with his characteristic smile. Kissing my forehead he handed me a present, saying in his booming baritone, 'This is what you get this time'. To my astonishment, I found that it was the pen that he had got as a gift from my grandmother, something that was immensely precious to him. I had always secretly admired it as a kid thinking that this was some 'special pen' that Baba wrote his scripts with! Though I had carried it with me to almost every part of the globe, I still haven't gathered the courage to use it!! At another occasion, when he missed his wedding anniversary at home due to a re-scheduled connecting flight back from Ootacamund races, he got an entire rose garden flown in with the pick of the best of rose blossoms from Bangalore and Ooty, as a form of apology for my mom. A famous actor, a part of Baba's repertory and trained by him, still recalls how Baba insisted and forced him to give up smoking after he found out that the actor got into the serious addiction after being introduced to it just for a scene which demanded smoking in one of his plays. Baba's collection of my grandfather's pipes and lighters, and his polo gear is again something invaluable for me.

My childhood impressions: an ode to motherhood

My early impressions as a child and the environment I grew up in, are from the historic Ahmed Bowla Bagh Palace on the outskirts of the city where I was born and spent my initial formative years. The imposing hundred-and-fifty-year-old structure, right in the middle of over a hundred-acre expanse of land, had an equally imposing granite staircase leading up to the first floor. The corniced terrace-top provided a breathtaking view of the city and a look from any of the verandahs gave you the look of a mini township that was our home. Mango groves, a fig orchard, a vineyard, rabbits, swans, a bird sanctuary, an arched pavilion for live concerts around a deep waterbody (a huge square shaped open well, recorded in the archives as the biggest *bowli* in the state, which gave the palace the name *bowla* in the local lingo) and a rose garden for mom on one side, poultry and dairy farms and the sub-continent's second largest stud farm on the other. The entire landscape, like our childhood, was cut off from the rest of world by a never-ending fortress-like boundary wall with two Victorian style gates on two different sides displaying an official 'No Horn Zone' sign engraved on it. So, as a toddler I and my two brothers got to play more with polo ponies than with children our age. We grew up learning to live in splendorous solitude instead of a normal childhood, waiting for those short-lived, stolen moments when we would sneak out into servant quarters, escaping momentarily from our *ayaahs* (governess), to find 'friends' our age. On the way back every Sunday afternoon we would keep count of the three hundred odd mango trees and over a hundred horses, believing innocently that they would multiply every week!

An endearing childhood memory that got stronger as I grew up, to the extent that it resulted in some memorable sequences in my work, both on in ad-films and on stage, is of my learning to walk, my nimble fingers clasping my mom's palm while climbing up the huge granite staircase that led to our bed chambers. Embedded images of this particular stairway can be seen when the man, embodiment of the conquering Indian spirit, scales the might of the Pyramids in Egypt with a mile-long satin flag and surrealistically lands on the Great Wall of China to the strains of *Vande Mataram* in the epic ad film. The opening sequence of 'Taramati-The Legend of an Artist' where Taramati in her flowing, beige tissue-brocade costume walks up the stairway of the historic Baradari to the tune of *'Piya baaj pyaala piya jaaye na...'* and in the end, walks into eternity beyond the same set of stairs. In 'His Exalted Highness' when the imaginary 'Hyderabad' descends on stage walking down the steps of the Chowmohalla Palace at the end of the number 'Yeh Hyderabad hai dosto...'. These scenes are images of an overweight toddler clasping his dainty mother's hand who, grace and elegance personified, taught him to walk and climb up the mighty stairway at home ... a tough task for him then. I still bank on her to walk me up emotional stairways. While the ad film *Vande Matram* is a salute to mother and motherland, 'Taramati' is an ode to womanhood. Incidentally, most of my later work is woman-centric. I did not realise it myself until someone from the local press asked me the reason. It is probably because after Baba's demise, Ammi has been the singular most influencing factor in my growing years. My reverence for her is not just for a wonderful mother but for a completely selfless person who was barely out of her teens when she got married and came into this ivory-towered household of three women; my grandmother, great grandmother and great grandma's mother, managed a domestic and stud farm staff of seventy five plus, played the perfect '*Dulhan Pasha*' while getting conditioned to a life where the next neighbour or an illuminated lamp was five-kilometre-radius away. Her sense of aesthetics and compassionate nature gave the very feudal house the warmth of a home and I always adored her organisational abilities like how at a very short notice she could arrange a grand hi-tea for guests, be it artists or visiting state dignitaries, sometimes as many as a few scores of them.

I still wonder whether her great culinary skills were inspired by Baba's spectacular theatre or his theatre was motivated by her skills. At an age when most girls today would just finish studies and begin to think of either settling down or working, she was already a mother of three brats. With changing times and political scenario, the family had to move out of Ahmed Bagh, and let go off it, and moved into another ancestral place in Murad Nagar. She coped up with it with equal dignity, at the same time, providing her unconditional support to Baba's legendary theatre movement and offered Hyderabad's theatre audience memorable adaptations of Tendulkar, Rakesh, Sarkar, Mitra and others. After Baba's demise, she grew multifold in her mental strength knowing well that she had to be both the parents to her growing kids. And what a wonderful 'set of parents' she has been to us! Salutation through my work is the least I can do to acknowledge her invaluable role in the family's and Hyderabad's theatre evolution. From nursing physical bruises of a spoilt brat to taking care of emotional scars of a growing adult, she did it all with equal dignity; someone who could be your best friend and your worst critic, a guide and a parent, all unconditionally. With a mum like her, a son like me would take pride in being called a mama's boy!

Courtesans, Palaces & Monuments of Hyderabad

Narendra Luther

Once upon a time there used to be kings and nobles—and their subjects. They typified the feudal system which was abolished in my lifetime. Palaces were the abode of royalty and nobility. The rulers had wives as a matter of course—and convention. They were acquired largely for political reasons, to strengthen military alliances, or as war booty. They were also necessary to continue the family line. To provide diversion from the routine of marital life, there were concubines, mistresses and courtesans who were experts in the art of seduction.

Muslim rulers institutionalised the practice of keeping women as objects of pleasure. After their satiation, they discarded the 'used' female objects across a wall of their 'harem'. While the ruler turned to the new object of desire, the discards were kept in a compound closely guarded by eunuchs so that, condemned to live on the memories of their all-too-brief pleasures, they could not do any mischief.

Courtesans were constant add-ons for the ruling class. They used to embellish the palaces and deodis with their alluring presence. They came and went and seldom became a permanent liability for their patrons.

The Founder Mistress

Hyderabad was no exception to this general pattern. In fact, its origin is credited to a courtesan. Its founder, Mohammad Quli Qutb Shah, as a teenage prince fell in love with a young accomplished singer and dancer, Bhagmati. She conquered the heart of the prince and proved an exception to the rule of temporary alliances by remaining the first and foremost of his ladyloves till the end of her days. Ferishta, the historian said in 1609 that the Sultan of Golconda was very fond of his mistress who visited him in great pomp.

Faizi, the Mughal Resident at the court of Ahmednagar (circa 1590-1594), reported to Emperor Akbar about the sultan's excessive fondness for 'the old whore'. Queen or courtesan, she has the distinction of having the new city named after her as Bhagyanagar, later called Hyderabad.

Abdullah, the grandson of the founder of Hyderabad, was the last but one ruler of the Qutb Shahi dynasty. Born in 1614, he became a ruler at the age of twelve and ruled till 1676.

Abdullah liked wine, women and song. His favourite mistress was Taramati whom he described as 'a flower from heaven'. He built a Baradari (a special pavilion having twelve open doors for fresh air) for her about a mile away from the Fort. She danced and sang only for him and it is said that he could hear her sing from her Baradari. Popular lore has it that on moonlit nights, she would sing and dance all the way to the fort on a ropeway.

In one of his poems he says about Taramati:

> *Yo lochan, yo joban, yo gaalaan, yo hontaan*
> *Hamin us ke aashiq, yo haq hai hamaraa*

(Her youth, those eyes, cheeks, and lips
I am her lover; they belong to me)

The Qutb Shahi dynasty ended in 1687 when Aurangzeb conquered Golconda and incorporated it in the Deccan province of the Mughal Empire.

Mah Laqa Bai Chanda

During the Asaf Jahi period a full-blooded courtesan, Mah Laqa Bai Chanda, came upon the scene in Hyderabad. She hailed from a good family, which, having fallen upon sad times moved to Hyderabad and took upon singing and dancing. Chanda was born in 1777 and was adopted by the child-less Rukunudoula, Dewan of the Nizam (1765-75). Besides singing and dancing, she studied history and poetry and became a good rider.

Her epitaph describes her as the 'cypress of grace and rosebush of the grove of coquetry'. That combined with her ready wit made her the darling of the second Nizam. He took her along on his military campaigns to Pangal and Nirmal and conferred the title of 'Mah Laqa' (Moon-faced) on her. Two successive Dewans of the two Nizams—Arastu Jah (1797-1804) and Mir Alam (1704-08) were stricken by her. She even played a crucial rule in the appointment of Chandu Lal (1832-42) as Dewan.

Raja Rambha Rao, a noble, sponsored the publication of her anthology in 1798 making her the first female published poet of Urdu. She wrote 125 ghazals of five couplets each. They are marked by a rare boldness for a woman. A sample:

Aap gardan to hilaa deteyn hain har baat par
Yeh ghazab hai keh machal jaaten hain phir ghaat par

(You so readily agree to whatever I propose
Coming to crunch, you are quick to dispose)

She set up a *taifa* to coach young girls in her line. Some of the famous courtesans and dancers of later generations came from there. She had extensive *jagirs* and died a rich woman known for her charity. She was buried in a tomb built by herself near the *dargah* of Maula Ali.

Strictly speaking, Khairunissa should not fall into this category, but she ended up as a mistress. A woman of extraordinary beauty, she was a grand niece of Mir Alam who later became Dewan of Hyderabad (1804-08). She was to be married to a much older person. To escape that, she enticed Kirkpatrick, the Resident to Hyderabad (1798-1805). He married her in 1800. It raised a storm but was tidied over.

Kirkpatrick died after five years making Khairunissa a widow at the age of nineteen. Soon thereafter, she became a lover of Henry Russell, her husband's assistant, and later a Resident himself. The affair lasted a year. While Russell married another woman, she was forced by Mir Alam to live in exile in Machilipatnam until after his death. She died in 1813, aged twenty-seven.

Palaces & Mansions

The founder of Hyderabad built fourteen palaces. He gave them fancy poetic but functional names like Dad Mahal, Sajan Mahal, and Nadi Mahal, etc. He himself stayed in the Qutb Mandir Palace. Only women attended the functions held there.

Some palaces were eight-storey high and had roof gardens, drawing praise from European visitors. His successors added some more. Even Aurangazeb was struck by the height and grandeur of the palaces. Most of them were destroyed during the Mughal invasion and thereafter.

Nizam Salabat Jung (1751-62) built Chow Mohalla in 1756. It is a complex of four palaces which replicates the palace of the emperor of Iran. In the north was the Durbar Hall where the Nizam held state receptions and entertained the British governor generals. Like other properties of the Nizam, it fell into destitude after the Police Action. Princess Esra, the first wife of Mukarram Jah took up its renovation in 2001 which is still going on.

The Purani Haveli Palace was acquired and improved by the second Nizam in 1762. It is built in European style and its central building has beautiful period furniture. Some other buildings also were added to it later. The fifth, sixth and seventh Nizams were born here. The sixth Nizam, Mir Mahboob Ali Khan was a dandy and never wore the same dress twice. He therefore had a double-storey, seventry-three-metre long wardrobe—the longest in the world.

He built a number of palaces. When he came to inspect the Saifabad Palace near the Husain Sagar Lake in 1887, a chameleon crossed his path. It was considered inauspicious and was therefore abandoned. It was later used as the State Secretariat. Recently, its demolition was stayed by the High Court.

A palace built in Rajasthani style was constructed by the nobles of Hyderabad to be presented to the Nizam on the completion of forty years of his rule. He died before it was completed. It was then made into the Town Hall and now houses the State Assembly. Another palace, originally built for the Nizam's daughter as a Doll House in the Public Garden, was also abandoned. It was then converted into the State Museum.

The last Nizam, Mir Osman Ali Khan moved away from the old city and bought a mansion in the new city built by one, Kamal Khan. His initials 'KK' were inscribed over various parts of the building including the furniture. To overcome the problem, it was given the hybrid name of 'King Kothi'. The Nizam lived there till his death in 1967. It is now in a dilapidated condition.

The Paigahs were the highest order of nobility under the Nizams. They were the only family with which the Nizams intermarried. They also built numerous palaces and deodis. The most famous, the Falaknuma Palace, was built by Nawab Viqar-ul-Umra in late nineteenth century.

On his visit to the palace, the Nizam praised it. It was promptly presented to him. It has a commanding view of the surroundings and has a priceless collection of paintings, jade statues and English furniture. Nobody lower in stature than the Viceroys of India ever stayed there. The sixth Nizam died there after he had a spat with his wife and went into a binge. Now a leading group of hotels has acquired it to be turned into a hotel.

The 'Bella Vista' was the residence of the Prince of Berar (crown prince) who was bypassed for succession. After serving for sometime as the State Guest House, it now houses the Administrative Staff College of India. The younger prince stayed in the Hill Fort Palace built in 1915 by Sir Nizamat Jung, a distinguished civil servant of the last Nizam. After the Police Action, it was converted into Ritz Hotel, and was the only 'modern' hotel in Hyderabad for a long time. Now it is lying vacant awaiting a decision of the government about its fate.

Other important palaces were the Asmangarh Palace, the Basheerbagh Palace, and the Chiran Palace.

The palaces built by lesser nobles were called 'havelis' or 'deodis' (mansions). The Malwala Palace was the best amongst them. The Diwan Deodi—the palace of the Salar Jung family later housed the famed one-man collection of the third Salar Jung. Subsequently, the deodi was demolished and the collection moved into a new building.

Two Paigah palaces have been partially converted into clubs—the Country Club and the Chiran Club. Most others have been razed to the ground to make way for commercial high-rise buildings.

Irram Manzil (Heavenly Abode) was another magnificent palace built by a noble called Fakhurul Mulk. It was subjected to the ultimate ignominy of being converted into the offices of the Irrigation, Buildings and Roads Departments of the government. It is now almost unrecognisable.

When the Residency was built in 1805, it was considered the most imposing British building in India next only to the Governor General's House in Kolkata. Now it houses the University College for Women.

Once the old city was dotted with havelis and deodis. Now only the remnants and ruins of a few can be seen. With their disappearance a complete way of life has vanished.

Monuments—Old & New

The Golconda Fort heads the hardy list of diminishing monuments. Originally a mud fort, built about 700 years ago, it was strengthened with stone and mortar in the sixteenth century. Its water supply system and acoustics are marvels of engineering. It fell into disuse in the nineteenth century.

The Sound & Light Show at the fort is a great tourist attraction. Close by, the Qutb Shahi necropolis is a resting place for the entire dynasty. It contains the grand mausoleum of the founder of the city. A lesser known building is the small mosque at the foot of the tomb of Hayat Bakshi Begum. Aurangzeb built it during the siege of Golconda rejecting the existing ornate mosque because its façade contained some un-Islamic motifs.

Exactly eight kilometres from the fort in a straight line towards the east stands the famed city centre of Hyderabad—

The Charminar

the Charminar. It was the very first building constructed when the city was founded in 1591. It is a perfect square with each side measuring 18.26 metres. Its four minarets rise to a height of 48.7 metres and each is divided into four storeys. A flight of 146 steps leads to the top storey. Not many people know that on the western side of its roof is a small mosque to accommodate forty-five people for prayer. Four roads radiated from Charminar in the four cardinal directions leading to different parts of the Golconda sultanate.

This monument has braved the noise and chemical pollution of incessant, increasing traffic for a long time. Now the area around it is being pedestrianised.

To the north of Charminar stands the Mecca Masjid, the second largest mosque in India. Its foundation was laid in 1617 by the sultan who claimed he had never missed any of the four daily prayers prescribed in Islam. It took more than seventy years to complete. Except the first and the last, all the Nizams are buried in its compound. There is a bench in the compound and it is believed that if a visitor to the city sits on it, he comes back—often to settle down in the city. There is no dearth of people who will vouch for that—including this author.

Tombs of the Paigah nobles on the road to the Santosh Nagar Colony are masterpieces of marble trelliswork constructed in the Rajasthani style. These tombs are without roof—according to strict Islamic injunction.

Monsieur Raymond (1755-98), the dashing last French commander of the troops of the second Nizam, was so popular that his name was corrupted into Musa Ram. He was buried on the road to Vijayawada on an elevated site with a good view. It has a seven metre conical obelisk. The locality is still called Musa Ram Bagh. Till mid-twentieth century an annual *urs* used to be held there in his memory. Now buildings on all sides have surrounded the tomb and it is not easy to locate it.

The city abounds in lesser known monuments. Secunderabad, the twin of Hyderabad has its own share of monuments like Maula Ali and the cantonment with the little known Military Jail and the house in which Winston Churchill stayed in 1885.

There is another unique monument—the rocks of Hyderabad. With fantastic shapes and considerable ecological value, they are a 2,500 million year old natural heritage. The government has notified nine of them as heritage precincts, but has not taken any steps to protect them from destruction.

Bhayagnagar became Hyderabad. Secunderabad was added to it at the close of eighteenth century. The latest urban focal point now is Cyberabad created in the last decade of the twentieth century. Located on the west of Jubilee Hills, this new suburb symbolises the future. With multinational corporates all around, it caters to a new generation for whom the world is a global family. No visit to Hyderabad is complete without seeing the new monuments there, like the Hi-Tec City Tower, The Indian School of Business, International IIT, and those that keep on coming up every other day.

Hyderabadi Cuisine

Pratibha Karan

Elizabeth Barret Browning, in a beautiful poem, wrote of Robert Browning, her husband:

> *How do I love thee let me count the ways.*

I can perhaps say the same of Hyderabad—the countless reasons why I love it.

There are many things that bind you to a place, not just its culture, its language or its cuisine. Even the ambience of a place, like its air, its water and its breeze bind you. You have to know Hyderabad intimately to fall in love with it. *Azaan*, the call for prayers one frequently hears in the city during the day, too has something so evocative and soulful about it, as though it is a part of Hyderabad's soul. Or take the Muslim holy month of Ramazan, when exotic food stalls mushroom all over the city, offering *Nehari* for *Sehri* (a pre-dawn meal) and *haleem* for *iftaar* (the post-dusk fast-breaking meal).

Hyderabad is a very plural city. It is a synthesis of many cultures living in harmony. Just like the people and the language of Hyderabad, there is something pluralistic and gracious about Hyderabadi food. It is very much like the Dakhni (Southern) Urdu which the Hyderabadi speaks, with lots of Persian, Arabic, Telugu and Marathi words thrown in. Savouring it amounts to a cultural experience. It is a mix of several influences, both Indian and foreign, but with a compelling identity all its own. It blends the class and refinement of the Mughal north with the sauce and spice of the south. Other influences have come from the Persians and the Arabs who came and settled in Hyderabad and from nearby Maharashtra and Karnataka. But most of all from the Telugus—the local people of the region. It is the Telugu cuisine that has contributed most to the tang and perkiness of Hyderabadi food.

Again, Hyderabadi food is not just *Biryani* and *Haleem* or *Baghare Baingan* and *Tomato Kut*. The repertoire is rich and vast both in vegetarian and non-vegetarian fare. Though admittedly, the fare is predominantly non-vegetarian. However, vegetables are added in most meat dishes and curries, barring the *biryanis* and the *kababs* and a few other non-vegetarian dishes. You have the *arbi* (colocasia) *bhindi* (okra) and *tori* (ribbed gourd) *ka shorva*, there is *tori-methi ka gosht* (ribbed gourd with fenugreek and meat), chicken made with *ambada* (roselle leaves) and then again chicken with *methi* and tomato. There is a rather nice dish called *chowgra*—meat made with several seasonal vegetables. Then there are the famous *Dulmas*—tomatoes, onions, or even apples and guavas, their core scooped out and then stuffed with *kheema*—akin to the *dolmas* of Greece and Armenia.

Whether by evolution or adoption (of the Western ways), the Hyderabadi also has his meals in courses. First comes the *gazak*, a starter that could be a *kabab* or a savoury or a patty. Then comes the *khaliya*, a dryish meat dish taken with a *phulka*. The last course consists of a *shorva* (a soupy meat dish) taken with rice. A *dal* (lentil) is also served as an option.

The array of meat and chicken curries are the pride of Hyderabadi cuisine. And unlike the North, where almost every non-vegetarian dish is just mutton curry or chicken curry, in Hyderabad every dish has its own character and a name to distinguish it from others. Thus, we have, to name just a few, *Salim Ram, Ananas ki Boti, Bhindi ka Shorva, Chigur Gosht, Nalli ka Khorma, Achari Murgh, Murg Methi* and so on.

The grandeur of Hyderabadi cuisine finds true expression in its *pulaos* and *biryanis*. It is said that around forty varieties of *biryani* are made in Hyderabad, which must include the *pulaos*. Some are delicate in taste, some intoxicatingly aromatic,

Cooking Biryani

some are flavoured with saffron, some with cream and milk and some others with rose water or screw pine flower water. One exceptional *pulao* is made of bone marrow. All these rice dishes can be made with lamb or beef. Chicken can also be used in place of mutton.

Biryanis are normally accompanied with *churri,* a relish of yoghurt, onions and some greens. *Churri* is called *Pachri* in other parts of Southern India.

Hyderabadi cuisine thoroughly exploits the versatility of minced meat and uses it in myriad ways. Minced meat cooked with vegetables such as cabbage, cauliflower, brinjal, tomato or potato forms part of the daily menu in Hyderabadi homes. Mince dishes can be cooked dry or with slight gravy and go well with Indian breads or rice. Several snacks and savouries are also made with mince as the main ingredient.

Several *kababs* too are made of mince. Mince flavoured with cassia buds and tenderised with papaya acquires an irresistible *kabab*-like flavour though it is not made like the kabab. It is called *Dum ka Kheema.* One baked dish, called *dum ke laoz* or *kheeme ki barfi,* has the look of an Indian sweetmeat but of course has the flavour of a unique kabab.

The Hyderabadi vegetarian dishes have a sparkling and lively quality. While some are simple but irresistible, others are rich. While we have the classic *Baghare Baigan, Mirchi ka Salan* and *Tomato Kut* without which Hyderabadi cuisine would be incomplete, there are other equally nice, though less famous dishes such as *Pyaz ki Tarkari, Dum ke Boot, Ambada Chana, Chowgra* and so on and so forth which so richly add to the repertoire of Hyderabadi cuisine.

Dals in Hyderabad come in several delicious varieties—another highlight of Hyderabadi cuisine. There are *Meethi Dals* and *Khatti Dals.* Then there is *dalcha* with mutton or vegetables like drumstick or bell peppers. We have the rare *Chironji ka*

Dalcha and a mix of several *dals* called *Keoti Dal*. A very special flavour is imparted to these *dals* with the typical Hyderabadi *baghar*—using preferably ghee and not oil and the Hyderabadi whole red hot chilli. It is said that one Prime Minister of Hyderabad, who was fond of cooking, could cook dals in fifty-two different ways.

What also distinguishes Hyderabadi food is its sourness, clearly a Telugu influence. A large variety of souring agents are used to enhance the flavours. They include not just lemon and tamarind but also vinegar, yoghurt, tomato, green mango, sour citrus, dried mango powder, fresh tamarind shoots and a sour leaf called *ambada* (roselle leaves). *Ambada* is a great favourite of the Hyderabadi. Fresh or dried prawns, chicken or meat cooked with *ambada* can be quite irresistible. The common dal (lentil curry) soured gently with *ambada* can be extraordinarily delicious. Then there are sour berries like the *karonda* (carissa caranda) and the *halfaleori* and the sour fruit like the *bilamboo* and the *kamrak* (star fruit) which too are used to sour meat dishes or make pickles. Star fruit pickle is not only most appetising but also visually attractive.

In fact, several Hyderabadi dishes are pickle-like in taste. So we have dishes like *Chatni Gosht*, *Achar Gosht* and *Achaar ke Aloo*.

Herbs and spices are the glory of Indian food and India has them in abundance. While most dishes in India are cooked with standard spices like ginger, garlic, cinnamon, cardamom and cloves, Hyderabadi cuisine can boast of some rather exotic spices. One *masala*, called the *Potli ka Masala*, consists of spices like sandalwood powder, khus and dried rose petals. These spices, in right proportions, are tied up in a *potli* (a small muslin cloth bag) and inserted into the dish while cooking. The *Potli ka Masala* is used mostly in *Nehari*, a broth of trotters and goat's tongue and in *chakna*, a tavern dish of meat and organ meat. This *masala* is quite unique in taste and is an orchestra of fragrances.

Bhojwar masala is another magical mix of various herbs and spices and is used in dishes like *Baghare Baigan*, *Mirchi ka Salan* and *Mahi Gosht*. It contains coriander seeds, sesame seeds, cumin seeds, bay leaf, copra and a lichen with an exotic aroma called *pathar ka phool*.

Hyderabadi food is mainly non-vegetarian with an evident bias for goat's meat—a clear Muslim influence. So while there is a wide range of mutton dishes, the fare is relatively limited in respect of fish, chicken or prawn. The Hyderabadi is also choosy about the meat and portions and cuts are carefully selected to suit the kind of dish being made.

Hyderabadi food is also generally hot and spicy—again a Telugu influence. The aromatic sting of red hot chilli, when inhaled or savoured, especially in *baghar*, the twang of black pepper both as corn and powdered, and the richness of red chilli powder or green chilli paste are features that distinguish Hyderabadi cuisine from other cuisines and make it heady and irresistible. Chillies are used in Hyderabadi cooking in many ways—chopped, ground into paste, slit, deseeded, or whole chillies, green or red, inserted into the dish. Sometimes, seeds of dry red chillies are collected and used after grinding.

In any cooking, it is important to have a delicate and balanced mix of spices because, if overdone, spices can ruin a dish. Therefore, spices are used in Hyderabadi cuisine in perfect balance and often, a single spice is used to bring out the exotic flavour of that specific spice or herb in a dish. So *khorma* is made using red chilli, *karai ka gosht* or *dum ka murgh* are made with green chilli. Then we have the pepper chicken using freshly ground peppercorn. There is also *chakna*, made in wayside taverns and patronised by the common people, which sometimes is finally sprinkled with powdered heads of cloves (forming the top round part of a clove). What is also kept in mind is that the spices do not dominate a dish but enhance its original flavour. Also the flavour of extra chillies and spices is, wherever required, neutralised by the use of yoghurt and other souring agents such as lemon, tamarind, *ambada*, green mango and the *ghee* in *baghar*.

The repertoire of sweet dishes in Hyderabadi cuisine is not so vast. Yet there are a few exotic sweets like the *Doodh Puri*, a thin silvery slice of mildly sweetened cream pancake arranged on a dry leaf and topped with *chandi ka wark* (silver leaf), and *badam ki jaali*, a delicate thin cake made of almond and cut into small filigree patterns. Then there are the celebrated *Khubani ka Meetha* (apricot and cream) *Double ka Meetha* (Indian bread pudding) and the sublime *Nimish* in which clouds of creamy foam are collected in earthen saucers.

I discovered rather early that to a Hyderabadi, good food is a passion and an obsession. Food is indeed viewed as a celebration and is prepared and eaten with much fuss, ceremony and elegance, especially during important occasions. As they say, the best food comes with *fursat* which means leisure, and *mohabbat* which means love.

Hyderabad is a city born in love. It was Mohammed Quli, who created the city of Hyderabad. His first love was a Hindu woman named Bhagmati, older than him and a courtesan of great fame and beauty. He eventually married her, gave her the honorific of Queen Hyder Mahal and named the city Hyderabad, after her.

The colourful city around Charminar, with shops selling jewellery, rare Basra pearls, and perfumery stores, bangle shops and *patang* (kite) shops, has never ceased to fascinate me. Not too far away are the Deodis (the palaces of the nobility). Then there are the *kabab* stalls of Machli Kaman. The aroma of *kababs* wafts through the city in the evenings just as a gentle breeze seems to often swing the city.

I associate Hyderabad with temperate climate, beautiful lakes and gentle and cool breezes. I also associate Hyderabad with sensuous evenings and nights spent on terraces with jasmine, *juhi* and *chameli* flowers. And on special occasions, with Aziz Ahmed Warsi singing his beautiful Qawallis, my favourite being:

> *Do badan pyar ki aag me jal gaye,*
> *Ek chameli ke mandway talay*

(written by the noted Hyderabadi poet,
Maqdoom Mohiuddin)

The evenings would be complete only with good wines flowing and the expectation of the most wonderful Hyderabadi cuisine.

Sports in Hyderabad

G. Rajaraman

I just have to hear the words 'once upon a time in Hyderabad' for my grandparents' voices to come wafting in. My brothers and I grew up listening to the many moral tales that grandfather, a retired postmaster, had up his sleeve each evening but my grandmother mostly recounted stories about Hyderabad. I can recollect her voice quivering every time she recalled the advent of plague and how she had to move her brood to a camp in Punjagutta. And, for that matter, when she told us with pride about how grandfather braved the Razakars during the Police Action in 1948 and guarded a sackful of cash to be able to turn it over to Government of India Agent General K.M. Munshi.

Yet, when I think of sports in Hyderabad, it is my father who stands out as a rich tapestry of images float in my mind's eye. I can vividly remember holding my sports journalist father's fingers when being introduced to a variety of sports. From educating myself in the nuances of cricket at Fateh Maidan and posing for pictures with Sunil Gavaskar—when he came back after a successful tour in the West Indies and England in

1971—to watching diverse sports such as football at Gymkhana Ground, boxing in the Railway Recreation Ground and sailing on the Hussain Sagar lake made for a great childhood. Many enlightening conversations with him come flooding back to my consciousness. Why, even in the writing of this piece, he has been a great inspiration. Being N. Ganesan's son always opened innumerable doors, not the least when I returned from my desk job in Madras to Hyderabad as a Sports Reporter in 1986.

It seems like only yesterday that I left home but in reality it has been more than a decade and a half since I boarded the Andhra Pradesh Express at Nampally seeking greener pastures in Delhi. My heart still beats with pride each time I see a Hyderabadi sportsperson deliver his or her best at the national sports arena for India. The Hyderabadi flavour returns each time I meet a champion—young and old—from the twin-cities. Each time I chat with my friend Harsha Bhogle, the years seemed to pass by effortlessly. The romance with Hyderabad lingers on. They speak fondly about *Gandipet ka paani*, don't they?

Indeed, there are so many memories to choose from—my own experience both as a sportsman and a sports journalist—that one doesn't know where to start. Perhaps it is easy to begin at the beginning, in the cosmopolitan locality where I began and spent much of life till I moved out of Hyderabad. Vittalwadi is a crowded area in Narayanguda and had its own share of heroes living there. National table tennis champion K Ramakrishna was a resident for many years but that was some time before I became aware of the beauty of sport. And when I was growing up, with Nagesh Kukunoor far from becoming the celebrated filmmaker that he is now, the likes of table tennis player Y.D. Upendernath, basketball player Mark Flynn and, most importantly, cricketer Mohammed Azharuddin were marking themselves out as special talent.

The amazing Azharuddin was the one who went on to make waves at the highest level for more than a decade and a half until he was discredited in the match-fixing controversy in 2000. We had an up-and-down relationship as cricketer and journalist but we have been able to paper over the cracks to be able to stay on one another's phone book. I have many wonderful memories featuring Azharuddin but none more delightful than when I gate-crashed into Azhar's birthday lunch in February 1999, a day after Anil Kumble claimed all 10 Pakistan wickets in a Test innings at the Ferozshah Kotla in Delhi. I am sure it was my Hyderabadi connection that helped me gain access to a delicious lunch. He was easily the most adored batsman of his generation and even the advent of Sachin Tendulkar did not lure fans away from his elegance. I was not around in Hyderabad when Azharuddin arrived after scoring hundreds in each of his first three Test matches back in 1984-85. I watched him for the first time in Test cricket in the Tied Test in Madras but his elegant knock of 81 against New Zealand in Hyderabad in 1988 more than made up for the image that the debonair M.L. Jaisimha imposed on my impressionable mind at the Lal Bahadur Stadium nearly two decades earlier.

Jaisimha gave me one of my favourite leadership stories. Back in January 1976, he made the mistake of choosing to bat first against a Railway attack on a track that had some wet spots. Hyderabad was soon in trouble and Jaisimha declared after just 21 overs with the score at 50 for 8, Anil Mathur taking seven wickets. Hyderabad picked up seven Railway wickets for 67 before the visiting team staged a rally and finished with a lead of 220 runs in the first innings. Jaisimha's team then made 376 for eight in 105 overs to set Railways a 157-run target in three hours. Syed Abid Ali and P. Jyothi Prasad took five wickets each to bowl Railways out for 76 and pull off a dream win with minutes to spare. Only a brave captain would have risked a declaration before lunch on day one of the match.

One of my lasting regrets is being unable to help Jai (as Jaisimha was called by anyone who knew him) with his autobiography. It was in January 1998 that I visited him last in his Marredpally home. Towards the end of the conversation, he asked me if I would help him put his book together. And I told him that since I was leaving for Delhi in a couple of days, I would gladly take up his offer on my next trip. As destiny would have it, he passed away on 6 July the next year and I never got around to taking up what would have been an enjoyable, educative experience.

'Lazy Elegance' is what I may have suggested as the title of that book not just to symbolise the man but also the slightly laidback approach to sport in keeping with the ethos of the twin-cities. Jai will remain the first in a long list of wrist artists that I shall cherish as typically Hyderabadi. Azharuddin and V.V.S. Laxman spring to mind as do volleyball genius Abdul Basith, table tennis maestro Mir Khasim Ali, hockey star N. Mukesh Kumar and badminton ace Pullela Gopi Chand.

There can be little doubt that the sporting ethos of the twin-cities was built and reared by the annual coaching camps that the Municipal Corporation of Hyderabad—and more recently, the Sports Authority of Andhra Pradesh—conducts each summer. It was, and I bet still is, a marvellous sight to watch scores of youngsters learning the fundamentals of a sport of their choice. It is a sure method to woo the young but the challenge has always been to sustain their interest, more so in the contemporary times when the thrust is on academics alone—and on tracking televised sport.

Thanks to the advent and evolution of satellite television that bring spectacular and high-class football action home from Europe, Latin American and European players are the modern day heroes for the youngsters in the twin-cities. It would be a good wager that Hyderabad City Police and the names of players like S.K. Azizuddin, Noor Mohammed, T. Balaram, Peter Thangaraj, Mohammed Habib, Mohammed Akbar and Shabbir Ali do not ring a bell in most minds. Then again, unmindful of that, the legend of Hyderabad City Police lives on.

S.A. Fruval would have become the first Hyderabadi to go to the Olympic Games had he been able to raise finances to travel to Helsiniki with the Indian football team in 1952. Four years later, six men—Azizuddin, Mohammed Zulfiqaruddin, S.A. Latif, S.A. Salam, T Balaram and Ahmed Hussain—gained that distinction as India finished a creditable fourth in Melbourne.

Coached by the redoubtable S.A. Rahim—who is still regarded by the knowledgeable as the best Indian football coach—Hyderabad City Police consistently challenged the supremacy of Calcutta's Big Three. Mohun Bagan, East Bengal and Mohammedan Sporting found the Hyderabad outfit a tough nut to crack and between 1950 and 1963, the policemen won the Rovers Cup in Bombay as many as nine times and the Durand Cup in Delhi four times. As several writers would testify, the team was identified as the side of the common man as opposed to the cash rich clubs of Calcutta. Its popularity transcended regional barriers quite easily.

One incident from 1950 will illustrate that amply. Hyderabad City Police was trailing Mohun Bagan by two goals in the Durand Cup final in Delhi but the team fought back to draw the game and earn a replay. Thousands of fans invaded the ground and Laiq, who scored the equalisier, was chaired into the team's change room. Some football lovers kissed him and one very excited fan even bit him and left Laiq bleeding from his cheeks.

One man was central to such reverence and domination— Rahim. He had turned up for the two best clubs in the city, Merry Go Round and Qamar Club in the 1920s and 1930s when the patronage of royal families like the Nawab of Tarbund and Maharaja of Dhanrajgir helped spread the game in Hyderabad. He later went on to become Hyderabad Football Association Secretary, running it from 1943 till his death in 1963.

Rahim introduced tournaments like the Nizam Gold Cup and the Majeed Challenge Shield. A good indication of his vision and practical approach can be had from the fact that he conceived a non-dribbling tournament for youngsters to raise the standard of speed and one-touch playing style. He was twice coach of the Indian team that won Asian Games gold medals.

Sticking with sporting history from before my time, let us look at how Hyderabad's cricket came to be. Raja Lochan Chand was reported to be the first chief patron of the game in late nineteenth and early twentieth century Hyderabad established an early lead among India's princely states to embrace cricket. Nawab Basalat Jah Bahadur and Maharaj Kishen Prasad, the Dewan of Hyderabad, led the way. Nawab Behram-ud-Dowla and Nawab Moin-ud-Dowla followed suit in creating greater interest in the game by donating two priceless cups to be contested on an all-India level. The Behram-ud-Dowla Cup started in 1928 and proved to be a great success, becoming the second most important competition after the Quadrangular tournament. Raja Dhanrajir's team, with Prof D.B. Deodhar at the helm, won the trophy outright by winning the tournament three years in a row. It was then that Nawab Moin-ud-Dowla instituted another Gold Cup.

Thanks to the patronage and efforts of Nawab Moin-ud-Dowla, first class cricket came to Hyderabad in 1930-31 with the Moin-ud-Dowla Gold Cup. Three teams participated in the tournament. They were Hyderabad, Maharaj Kumar of Vizianagaram XI and Nawab of Moin-ud-Dowla XI. The fans witnessed world class players for the first time in MCC Test stars Jack Hobbs and Bert Sutcliffe. A number of famous Indian players like C.K. Nayudu, Wazir Ali, J.G. Nalve, Amar Singh and Naoomal Jaoomal who went on to represent India in the inaugural Test at Lord's in 1932 also turned up.

Of course, by the time I was a young lad, princely patronage of sport was a thing of the past and a company like Vazir Sultan Tobacco became the pioneer of corporate sponsorship in India. It was at this time that Hyderabad cricket flourished with as many as seven cricketers wearing India colours. Later, of course, when left-arm spinner Venkatapathi Raju made his debut, I wrote about how Hyderabad could boast of raising a well balanced team for India. The charming Abbas Ali Baig and K. Jayantilal as opening batsmen, Azharuddin, Mansur Ali Khan Pataudi, Jaisimha and V.V.S. Laxman would form a sensational middle-order. Leg-spinning all-rounder M.V. Narasimha Rao, wicket-keeper P. Krishnamurthy, medium fast bowler Syed Abid Ali would share the new ball along side Jaisimha while off-spinners of the class of Ghulam Ahmed, Shivlal Yadav and Arshad Ayub would fight for one spot.

The mention of Pataudi takes me back to a cherished story that has acquired cult status despite perhaps being apocryphal. Pataudi had problems with the office-bearers in Delhi and District Cricket Association and since he wasn't born in the twin-cities, he needed to find a job in Hyderabad to be able to play Ranji Trophy from 1965-66. His friend Jaisimha organised that by getting his father to 'employ' Pataudi on a token salary.

Any such walk down memory lane will be incomplete if I do not recall some sporting venues in the twin-cities. Much time may have passed—and the Musi may have become a drain—but images from Fateh Maidan will never acquire sepia tones. The last of the major events I watched at the Lal Bahadur Stadium was the Pre-Olympic football tournament in 1991 but I was privileged to witness many exciting Moin-ud-Dowla Gold Cup, Ranji Trophy and Duleep Trophy matches. I do not remember watching a football game in the famed Gosha Mahal Stadium, home of the Hyderabad City Police team. More often than not, circus tents would be pitched there but I remember dad talking nostalgically about Rahim and his team training there. Of course, I also remember going to a shotgun competition there.

I am not sure if it has survived the ravages of commercialisation of education. But the cricket ground in Aizza High School, Malakpet, will be a very special cricket ground in my life. It was the venue of my only inter-school cricket match. Some of my schoolmates and I mustered courage to convince our school Principal S. Udapachar that we needed to enter our cricket team in inter-school tournament so that we could further our talents. And in our final year of school, we managed to convince the stern soul that sports could also help build character. And as our luck would have it, we drew All Saints High School in our opening round Basalt Jah Trophy game. Abdul Azeem, later to scintillate as opener for Hyderabad in Ranji Trophy, demolished our dreams with a magnificent century, leaving us licking our wounds.

The other ground that I remember from my childhood was a sprawling area called the Chintal Thota—or Imli Bagh—in Lingampally. As members of the Friends CC or Youngsters Sports Club, we used to walk some distance to play our own weekly Tests against a team from the neighbouring Venkateshwara Colony. It has now disappeared and blocks of apartments have sprung up in its place. Similarly, each time we pass the Telephone Exchange in Musheerabad my father, a sports journalist and administrator in his time, speaks wistfully about the Mehdi Nawaz Jang tennis stadium that used to stand in its place. Mr Ganesan recalls how Ghaus Mohammed, the first Indian to enter the quarterfinals at Wimbledon, made Hyderabad his home.

YMCA is where I watched some great table tennis contests featuring the likes of Mir Khasim Ali, Yahya Khan, Subash Reddy and saw sisters B. Usha and B. Savitri dominate the women's events. YMCA would be so full of life on Independence Day when dawn-to-dusk competitions would be held in many disciplines, D.S. Chinnadorai and Egbert Samraj establishing a fine tradition of encouraging sport. At a time when chess had not caught the imagination of people, Nasiruddin Ghalib and his *ustaad* Mohammed Hassan were regulars at the YMCA. We would watch in awe as Ghalib, who won not a few awards of the best game at the National A Championship, and Hassan got immersed in a game.

I shall cherish my association with Ghalib, one of the bravest people I have met. Former India women's cricket captain Purnima Rau is another such personality. She overcame personal tragedy and gave expression of her character in the kind of intense cricket that she championed. There is a fairly long list of characters from Hyderabad sport that I can recall. Sayeeda Sultana, a national table tennis champion as well as cricketers Asif Iqbal and Waheed Yar Khan moved to Pakistan. Volleyball player Mulini Reddy became the first woman from the city to be honoured with the Arjuna Award while T. Gopal and Venkatnarayana were in the forefront of the volleyball bandwagon. Basketball stars Mohammed Rizwan and Hari Krishna Prasad played for India with distinction as did women cricketers Sandra Braganza and Ranjini Venugopal. Davis Cupper S.P. Misra and his brother S.S. Misra set the tone for other tennis players like S. Narendernath and Vasudeva Reddy. On the badminton court, Praveen Kumar and Manoj Kumar made a name for themselves as a champion doubles pair. Boxing coach E. Chiranjeevi did a stellar job of ensuring that the city would carry the tradition set by pugilists like Dennis Swamy, Saleem Siddiqui and Saad Farooqi. Rami Reddy, Krishna Bose and Dhanalakshmi came to the fore from track and field while cyclist Maxwell Trevor was quite unbeatable for some years. C.S. Pradeepak did well for himself as a champion sailor in a sport that was dominated by the Services. My friend

Suresh Kumar started off as a basketball player at Victory Play Ground but rose to lead the Indian handball team.

I cannot ever forget the day when Arjuna Award winning volleyball player Abdul Basith died of electrocution in 1991. I borrowed the following lines from a song in Raj Kapoor's *Mera Naam Joker* for use in the obituary:

> *Kal khel mein hum ho na ho,*
> *gardish mein sitare rahenge sada...*

Many of Hyderabad's heroes may have slipped from collective public consciousness but their contribution to Hyderabad and Indian sport at large cannot ever fade. Of course, there are others—V.V.S. Laxman, Sania Mirza, Saina Nehwal, Mitali Raj, Chetan Anand—who are in the process of adding to the pages of the twin-cities' sporting history. Some day, someone else would sit down with a cup of Irani *chai* and start by saying, 'Once Upon a Time in Hyderabad...'

The Deodis of Charminar

Rani Sarma

Uptil 1947, the old city of Hyderabad was home to powerful jagirdars (feudal lords) and nobles who lived in old style fortified residences called deodis. The basic concept of building deodis with large entrances, high walls and inner courtyards was prevalent in Marathwada and Telengana in the seventeenth and eighteenth centuries. The internecine clashes between the warring powers of the Deccan made security a major concern for the feudal lords and the deodis, with their high walls and inner spaces offered protection, not only to the feudal lord but also to his people in troubled times.

The first Nizam, Nizam-ul-mulk, ruled his territory with Aurangabad as his capital. It was in the year 1763 that the capital shifted to Hyderabad under Nawab Nizam Ali Khan, the second Nizam. The feudal lords and the nobles who followed the Nizam to Hyderabad brought with them the concept of building deodis from Marathwada. In Hyderabad they continued with the tradition of living in deodis.

In the city of Hyderabad, while the core features meant for security were retained, the deodis were enlarged and made more elaborate. The main entrances were made more intricate and the high walls of the deodi enclosed more spaces as the courtyards became more in number. Unlike the deodis of Marathwada, where security was the prime concern, in Hyderabad opulence, display of wealth and grandeur came to mark the dwellings of the nobles. There was a strict segregation of the living quarters of the men and the women of the deodis of Hyderabad. Men lived in mardanas and the women in zenanas. Over a period of time sundry structures like a jillu khana, diwan khana, aina khana, tosha khana, mez khana, farrash khana and a baggi khana were added to the deodi, necessitated by the life of luxury that the nobles lead. Deodis of the important nobles were built along the main arteries of the old city that radiated from Charminar. Living close to the palaces of the Nizam, like the Purani Haveli, Punch Mohalla and Chow Mohalla, was a mark of a noble's importance and social standing.

The entrances to the deodis were imposing and high enough to let an elephant with a hauda (which the feudal lord rode on ceremonial occasions) pass. The huge wooden doors of the gate were strengthened with iron knobs and spikes. Some deodis of important nobles had jillu khanas, where the guests alighted from their vehicles and were received, before being conducted into the deodi. Armed Sikhs, Rajputs or Arabs guarded the entrances. Naubat (music) played from the upper floors of the imposing entrance either to indicate the time of the day, to announce a special event within or to herald the arrival of a special guest. Naubat was a special privilege granted by the Nizam for meritorious services rendered.

Deodis of important nobles occupied whole streets and sometimes extended to the adjacent streets as well. They bore a drab look from outside and were sometimes surrounded by shops. However, the interiors of the deodi were decorated attractively and were in marked contrast with the exteriors. They were adorned with beautiful ornamental dalan, carved pillars, painted ceilings and multi-foliated Shahjahani arches; the walls were decorated with miniature paintings besides being equipped with a musnad for the owner of the deodi and takhats covered with expensive carpets for the guests. In later years they came to be further decorated with expensive furniture, chandeliers, art pieces and bric-a-brac, depending on the wealth and stature of the owner.

Deodis were in reality like self-contained townships; within the wall of each deodi lived the feudal lord and his extended family, his relatives and his dependents. In most cases the employees that provided day-to-day services to the deodi like

Diwan Deodi

servants, sweepers, palanquin bearers, sweepers, cooks and drivers too lived on the grounds, in large wadas.

An important addition to the deodis of Hyderabad was the baradari, literally the 'twelve doors'. The tradition of building baradaris came down to Hyderabad from the Qutubshahi days. The Taramati Baradari built at that time stands to the present day. Baradaris were generally built outside the city, in the middle of attractive gardens, or overlooking water bodies as they were the places where the nobles entertained their important male guests.

The tone of a deodi was set by its master. Some like the Diwan Deodi, Deodi Asman Jah, Peshkar Deodi, Rai Rayan Deodi and the deodi of the Malwalas buzzed with much activity. These nobles held important positions at the court of the Nizam and transacted business in their forecourts. The members of the Salar Jung family functioned as the Prime Ministers of the state while those of Chandulal-Kishen Pershad family were the traditional peshkars. The Rai Rayans and the Malwalas were daftardars in charge of tax collection. The large forecourts of all those deodis teemed with petitioners, officers, applicants, tax collectors, soldiers and chobdars. While the forecourt was used for official matters, the inner courts were used for private activities.

Unlike the mardana, where hectic official activity was visible, life in the zenana was relaxed and slow paced. The women of the zenana lived in strict purdah. The principal wives of the nobles at times had independent living quarters. A side gate, called the zenani darwaza gave access to the zenana and women security guards and female servants took care of its security. Immediately after the zenani gate was a large screen which provided further privacy to the ladies of the zenana. The interior of the lady's section had a series of courtyards inter-connected with passages at the back. Men were not permitted into the zenana and, on the occasion of a visit by a male member of the family, they had to be announced and the inmates alerted. There was only one entrance to the zenana and it was guarded zealously by a female servant of advanced years.

The interiors of the zenanas were beautiful, with flowering bushes, fruit-bearing trees, fountains and caged birds like mynas and lalmunias. They were attended to by hoardes of female servants and provided with every kind of luxury. Old faithful servants would take charge of the begum's wardrobe and jewellery. The begum of an important noble would surround herself with a pandan, itrdan, gulab pash, ugaldan and other articles of day to day use, all made in silver. Seated on an expensive carpet, leaning on a gau takia, she would hold court in the main dalan or a richly appointed hall of the zenana, with all the dignity and splendour that her position called for. The clothes that the women wore were most elaborate and expensive, made of the finest benarasi silk, himroo and mushajjar cloth. They wore jewellery literally from head to toe. Such a collection, which began with the tikka, worn on the parting of the hair, jhoomer, worn on the right side of one's head and ended with 'sone ke kabutar' which was an elaborate anklet made of Basra pearls, emeralds and uncut diamonds, was called a sarapa or saaz. Women seldom travelled outside the deodi, but on the rare occasions when they did move out, great excitement gripped the zenana. Preparations went on for days and large retinues travelled with the begums. Visits by women of other deodis were few but when they came, they stayed for days, not hours. Women spent most of the day in planning meals, in supervising jewellery making, overseeing karchob and zari kamdani and in offering prayers. Jewellers and artisans were attached to individual deodis, where they lived as long as there was work, which was almost always.

It is inside these deodis that the famous 'tehzeeb' of Hyderabad was born and nurtured. Refinement in the manner of greeting elders, equals and inferiors, the spoken language, the reception of guests, one's conduct in public were all matters of great importance and were taught to the children from an early age. Strict rules governed social conduct and no one, however important, was exempted. The Hyderabadi nobles formed a closed group, conscious of their superiority of birth and position at the court. They interacted and had social contact only with the families of similar standing. Over a period of time, complicated rules of etiquette evolved which assumed great importance in their social conduct. They inherited much of their courtly manners and etiquette from the Mughal Court. To that was added the local flavour passed down from the Qutub Shahis. Even the British had to be careful not to breach protocol, for any infringement of the tradition and convention was considered a slight and an intended insult to the dignity of a noble. The Hyderabadi nobles did not visit one another unless they were appropriately attired and even sons could not enter the presence of their parents unless they were properly dressed.

There is an interesting story, which illustrates the point. Once Maharaja Kishen Pershad, the hereditary peshkar and later the Prime Minister of the State of Hyderabad, who was considered to be the epitome of refinement, went calling on Khan Khannan, another premier noble, at his deodi. Khan Khannan waited at the portico appropriately dressed in the traditional dastar (head-dress) and bugloos (belt) to receive his guest. The Maharaja's motorcar drove up at the appointed time but instead of stopping at the portico, drove beyond. Every one present and in readiness to receive the Maharaja was astonished at this strange behaviour and breach of protocol. An officer jumped out of the escort car of the Maharaja and ran to him. Fierce whispers and consultations followed, as Khan Khannan watched perplexed. What had actually transpired was that the Maharaja had set out without wearing his traditional bugloos, and was mortified at the thought of appearing before Khan Khannan without it, insufficiently dressed as he was! The tricky situation was finally resolved when Khan Khannan decided to discard his bugloos and the two nobles were able to meet with appropriate courtesy to each other!

The Hyderabadi nobles lived extravagantly, their lifestyles rivaling even that of the ruler at times. Their homes were veritable treasure troves; large sums were spent on revelries, hunting parties, lavish banquets and in other forms of entertainment. The Nizam and his nobles kept the Mughal tradition of miniature paintings alive in Hyderabad while the others were patrons of art, music and poetry. Maharaja Kishen Pershad was a respected poet in his own right and patronised many young aspiring poets that flocked to him from all over the country. Salar Jungs were celebrated collectors of art and artifacts. Raja Sham Raj had a museum of artifacts in his deodi. Inayat Jung and Surai Yar Jung had excellent libraries. Mahmood Nawab Mahboob Ali Khan, whose pen name was 'Tairo' was a very talented painter. The tradition of qawwali was popular in Hyderabad and so were mushairas, which were held regularly in the deodis. Hyderabad developed its own distinct cuisine, dress, spoken language and marriage customs.

The premier nobles believed in being generous to a fault, in helping the poor and the needy. They vied with one another in being called as 'generous.' There would be a hoard of applicants at the deodis every day asking for help, donations, grants and so on, for a variety of needs like marriages, education, going on a pilgrimage to Mecca and so on. They seldom returned empty handed.

However, there was a darker side to the life in the deodis, which proved to be the undoing of the nobles, when jagirs were abolished in the year 1949. A majority of the nobles lived beyond their means and took no interest in administering their jagirs properly. They gathered around themselves coteries of sycophants and flatterers, who led them to believe that they had unlimited supply of money to spend. They led insular lives, removed from reality, clamoring for titles which were hollow and carried no real merit. Except for the begums of some famous families like the Salar Jungs, the women in the deodis were generally uneducated; they were superstitious and old fashioned in thinking and had to contend with neglect, boredom and jealousies.

With the arrival of the Europeans in Hyderabad and the subsequent signing of the Subsidiary Alliance in the year 1798, the epicentre of power shifted from the Nizam's court to the British Residency. The nobles were quick to realise that they had to be familiar with the western way of life so as to be acceptable to them socially. Consequently, the otherwise tradition loving nobles of Hyderabad started to imitate the Europeans in the manner of their dress, their eating habits and building their residences. Governesses were appointed to teach the children table manners and to speak English with the right intonation and idiom. Some of the children were sent to England to study there. However, even though the nobles acquired the trappings of western lifestyle, such influence was skin deep and they remained truly traditional and Hyderabadi at heart.

Unlike men, women rarely interacted with the Europeans. They stuck to their traditions. While the men employed Goanese cooks to dish out European food, the women continued to eat local Hyderabadi and Mughlai food. Eating was an elaborate ritual, a dastarkhan would be spread on the floor and the ladies sat around it; female servants poured warm water from an aftaba and the begums washed their hands in a sailafchi. The men too reverted to the traditional style of eating when they ate with their families.

With the construction of the British Residency in a Palladian style by 1806, ideas of modern living with facilities like plumbing came to the city. The old fashioned deodis, with their high walls and cramped surroundings lost their appeal. Natural disasters like the Musi flood of 1908 and the plague of 1911 also prompted the nobility to move away from the walled city. Nawab Mahboob Ali Khan, the sixth Nizam, built himself a modern mansion and a race course at Malakpet where he lived and later the seventh Nizam too moved to another residence called King Koti, across the river Musi in 1914. The nobles followed suit and those who could afford to, built second homes. They built modern palaces set in large gardens, in areas like Khairatabad, Sarur Nagar and Malakpet. Some like the Rai Rayans, added clocks on the entrances of their deodis in the old city as a token of modernity while some others, like the Paigahs and Malwalas added whole blocks of modern structures, complete with reception rooms to receive their European visitors.

However, it is interesting to note that even though the Hyderabadis moved away from the traditional deodis, they retained some traditional elements of the deodis like building baradaris and separate zenanas even in their modern homes. For those that moved to their new mansions, it did not make economic sense to spend money on the ramshackle old deodis. Slowly, the once fabulous deodis started to decay and turned dilapidated.

The integration of the State of Hyderabad in 1948 with the rest of India and the subsequent abolition of the jagirs in 1949 dismantled the feudal base of Hyderabad. The few deodis that survived these cataclysmic events (as the nobility viewed them) finally fell to the Urban Land Ceiling Act of 1976. With the main source of their incomes having dried up, properties had to be divided between the heirs. Sometimes the valuable art pieces of the deodis were sold as a prelude to dividing the property. Art dealers and auctioneers roamed the city to buy back art of immense value at throwaway prices. Articles, which were once purchased at a great cost were sold for a song. Finally the deodis were demolished by the owners themselves and the land on which they stood was sold as small plots. The carved pillars and the painted woodwork that once adorned the deodis were sold as scrap.

Today, the few remaining deodis that still stand in their dilapidated form, function as schools or shadi khanas. Even the Nizam's Purani Haveli is stripped of its past majesty. Perhaps no other city in India lost as much built heritage as Hyderabad did in a very short span of time. The transformation of the old city is so complete that the visitors to the city are hard put to find any traces of the old grandeur. Driving past the old city's busy streets, one can still spot a few broken down arches and lonely looking gateways, full of character, looking incongruous in the new surroundings. They stand as poignant reminders of what could have been saved.

Healthcare Scenario in Hyderabad: Before and After Apollo

Sangita Reddy

The impetus for the establishment of Apollo Hospital in Hyderabad came from the serendipitous summit at Apollo Chennai (then Madras) between the late Shri T. Anjaiah Garu, former Chief Minister of Andhra Pradesh and my father, Dr Prathap C. Reddy. The Chief Minister Shri Garu was impressed by what he saw at Apollo Chennai and asked Dr Reddy to create a similar healthcare infrastructure in his home state of Andhra Pradesh. My father promptly replied, 'The people of Andhra Desam need good healthcare, I will be happy to do so'.

It was in 1984, when the Chief Minister Shri Anjaiah Garu offered a choice of two locations, one that was smaller and centrally located and the other in Jubilee Hills, then a hilly and sparsely populated community on the outer edge of Hyderabad. My father chose the thirty-three-acre land at Jubilee Hills. It was literally 'the road less travelled' on the outskirts of Hyderabad. I recall our competitors jokingly remarking, 'Patients would need a helicopter to get them to the hospital'.

For most people, the very idea of building a world-class tertiary care hospital in a setting which was at a fair distance from the population centre, more suitable for hiking, mountaineering, or wild game hunting, was inconceivable. While others saw the challenges in establishing the super-specialty hospital in a remote location as formidable and incomprehensible, my father perceived it as an opportunity. It is this foresight, long-term strategic thinking, and vision that never ceases to amaze me. He dreams of things that never were and asks why not?

In 1989, the largest private hospital in Hyderabad was the Hyderabad Nursing Home. Until that time, all other medium and large specialty hospitals in Mumbai and other cities were established by big business groups as trusts or societies and not as corporate entities. In this regard, Apollo Chennai and Apollo Hyderabad were India's first corporate hospitals. Thus, Apollo marked a change in the organisational form of private investment in healthcare. Over the next decade and a half, the success of the Apollo format, coupled with the change in the institutional funding act (once again at the behest of my father) catalised a shift from single owner enterprise and nursing homes to corporate enterprises.

During the 1980s, there were no corporate hospitals in India and consequently Apollo had to face many daunting challenges. Having no precedents, it was not a very viable idea. Furthermore, the country's administrative policies were not investment-friendly. Under these circumstances, building and managing a corporate hospital meant investing in expensive imported equipment, luring experienced doctors from abroad as well as recruiting available manpower for ancillary services, and last but not the least, providing hands-on training to meet the established Apollo standard of quality.

Another tangible factor was the cost of medical equipment; for a hundred-bed hospital it was approximately twenty-eight percent to thirty percent of the project cost. The accelerated obsolescence of the medical equipment combined with the high cost of maintenance to assure uptime added to the recurring cost. Due to father's advanced training at Harvard University hospitals and experience as a practicing physician in the US, he was familiar with the latest trends in medical technology and other essentials that he wanted the Apollo doctors to employ to provide the best patient care.

This benchmarking against the best hospitals in the world meant importing medical and surgical instruments, equipments, and disposables at the prevailing rate of customs duties. In the absence of any concessions in the forms of import duties and taxes, the task of managing a hospital became truly challenging! In spite of these and other formidable obstacles, Dad's resolve, determination, perseverance, and tenacity to bring world-class healthcare to Hyderabad became a reality in the form of Apollo Hyderabad.

Dad realised that a world-class hospital has to have a world-class team of medical practitioners. I fondly recall Dad's conversation with Dr M. R. Girinath, a legend in cardio-thoracic surgery at that time and Chief of Cardio-Thoracic Surgery at Apollo, Chennai. Dad requested Dr Girinath to recommend a surgeon who could replicate his success at Apollo Hyderabad. As it turned out, the recommended surgeon was not the one who was trained at any of the best hospitals abroad, but a member of his own Apollo Chennai team in Dr Vijay Dixit.

In concert with experience to date then, and even as of today, Dad's invitation to a dedicated professional to join the Apollo Family has always been honoured. The invitation to Dr Vijay Dixit was no exception. Accompanied with his wife Rita, the couple moved to Hyderabad and grew to love the 'City of Pearls'. With almost two decades of service to healing the sick in Hyderabad and over 15,000 heart operations, with outcome unmatched in the world, I believe Dr Dixit's move to Hyderabad was guided by a higher power. Besides this he was instrumental in bringing other local stalwarts like Dr Jairam Pingle, Dr Seshagiri (who was actually the first Cardiologist in Apollo, Chennai) to the Apollo family.

It is to Apollo Hyderabad's credit that several of our doctors have made a name for themselves through outstanding patient care. Our physicians have the clinical expertise, compassion, dedication, maintain high ethical standards, and are accessible. The highest quality of medical care at Apollo Hyderabad has been made possible because of our investment in the latest and cutting-edge technology, exemplary work environment, equal and fair treatment, and administration's undivided attention to the needs of the medical staff, patients, and other constituencies.

In the light of Apollo Hyderabad's reputation as a doctor-friendly hospital under Dad's stewardship, an increasing number of NRI physicians are joining the Apollo Family. Our retention rate is second to none in the world. Moreover, Apollo Hyderabad has been ranked in a national survey as the Best Hospital in Hyderabad.

On the eve of the Silver Jubilee of Apollo Hospitals Group, and on the sprawling thirty-three acre campus of Apollo Hyderabad, the erstwhile hilly, rocky, and deserted terrain saw the inauguration of Asia's First Health City. The Apollo Health City is constantly abuzz with activity, twenty-four hours a day! In addition to patient care, there are programmes geared towards integrated wellness services for children, senior citizens, as well as education, research, healthcare IT and BPO services in one location.

Over the past few decades, healthcare has progressed from structure, processes to outcome. Recent years have brought major changes in healthcare. The standalone institutions are passé and the future lies in alliances. The forms of alliances vary, but they are generally referred to as 'integrated delivery systems' because they bring together, or 'integrate' the components that provide healthcare into one 'full-service' healthcare delivery system.

Thanks to Dad's vision, Apollo has already made the move in the right direction and created the Integrated Healthcare Delivery System in the form of Apollo Health City Hyderabad. We are fully geared for the future. Apollo Health City Hyderabad has identified the relationship between the coordination of care provided and a successful transition experience meaning the consumer being able to function well at home. The Apollo Health City Model has a number of elements including: 1) the meaning of coordination to consumers; 2) the aspect of health system support that is important for coordination and for preparing the consumer to return home; and 3) the factors that contribute to a successful transition.

Dad has always believed in divine intervention that guides all our mortal decisions. Perhaps it was divine intervention all along that has guided Dad in abutting the wall of Apollo Hyderabad premises with a memorial built in honour of a Hakim. Legend has it that the place was actually the dwelling of the old mendicant. He was so famous that people from all over the Deccan Plateau visited this site to be cured of their ailments. Maybe it was the Hakim's spirit that guided us to Jubilee Hills to build a modern world-class healthcare institution. And if so, may that very same spirit of healing continue to guide us on.

Culinary Journey of Hyderabad

Shankar Krishnamurthy

My tryst with Hyderabad began in June 1996, when I moved in as the Executive Chef of Holiday Inn Krishna Hotel (now Taj Deccan). I had come from a very high paced, dynamic, and international cauldron of culinary delights—Dubai. I was in Dubai, at the best time of my life, getting exposed to varied cultures, foods, tastes and languages. Dubai then had already begun moving at a frenetic pace to catch up with the western world in all walks of life. Hyderabad on the other hand was snug in its time warped zones, where the nawabi lifestyles were still somewhat prevalent, just a few hotels ruled, and Indian and Chinese food ruled the roost.

As an energetic chef, I settled in quickly, bringing to Hyderabad the whole range of international food. At that time, it was happily accepted in parties, more as a change to the regular fare, and coupled with curiosity. It is now almost twelve years since I started that nouvelle cuisine and created many a successful, palate defining menus during my two-year stint there. After that I moved back to Dubai, and then went off for a stint at Nepal. It was finally in 2002 that I decided to hang my boots, and get into the entrepreneurship mode to open my own restaurant, a dream of every chef.

I was contemplating Bombay, Delhi, but wanted to check out Hyderabad as well, as my only stint in India over the last twelve years was here. I was also comfortable in Hyderabad because I knew a few good people, and this new adventure was an acid test for me.

In September 2002, I came to have a recce of Hyderabad from Katmandu. I went around the city, which had not changed much on the food front. New restaurants were operating, Chinese, Indian still ruled the roost, but there was a continental restaurant running too, without much ado. I met up with my friends, prominent people from the city's social scene and bounced the idea of starting a global cuisine restaurant. I was surprised at the strong backlash; they all said it was a bad idea as only Indian/Chinese restaurants would survive in Hyderabad. There were however a few encouraging voices too.

Soon I went around tasting, and sampling the local fare. There was a café, which had opened up, claiming to offer world cuisine. That was all to convince me of my concept restaurant and I decided to move in. I made my decision, went back to Katmandu, quit my job, and moved bag and baggage to Hyderabad. We were fortunate to get a good location on Road No 1, Banjara Hills and Fusion 9 was born.

We went about designing F9 in a very simple straight line two-tone restaurant. The décor was very understated, thereby completely different to what was offered in Hyderabad during those times. The central bar, split lounge seating, different level dining, was like a breath of fresh air to Hyderabad, which was used to flashy and ornate interiors. The menu was carefully worked around; I came up with a mix of cuisines I thought would work well in the city. I was targeting the fast developing

IT sector as also the fair traffic of expats growing by the day.

F9 opened its doors with great gusto. There were huge expectations all around. As it was run by a chef, so we had to get the food part right. All this was making me very jittery, but nervous energy luckily has always propelled me in the right directions. The start was promising, and we got the right mix of clientele. The location was fabulous too, sandwiched as it was between three five-star hotels. I received a ready response from the expats, which I felt was a very positive signal for change as far as Hyderabad cuisine was concerned. The expats loved F9, the media was helpful, and soon it was attracting celebrities as the word of mouth advertising was very strong. Fusion 9, the name, denoted a menu mix of nine international cuisines. I didn't tinker much with the food and served it the way it was supposed to be. This was a good move, I believe, as it offered something for everybody's palate. There was Chinese, Cuban, Vietnamese, French, Greek, Indian and so on.

F9 received a fair share of feedback on everything—food, service, ambience, et al. It soon became a favourite haunt for many. What was surprising was that it cut across all age groups, turning into a favourite food joint for the young as well as the old. Though I was targeting a thirty-plus age group, F9 developed its own soul.

There was a fair bit of education that went into the process. We were doing pre-plated food, which was also fairly new to the city, as they were used to sharing a dish. They used to find the quantity small on the plate, and had to be explained that the dish was meant for one person only. Then they used to wonder why the food was not spicy enough; I was clear not to dilute the food, in general, and prepared dishes as per their specific requirements.

The city always had Indians travelling in hoardes abroad, but somehow Indian and Chinese joints had maintained their monopoly. F9 changed this trend, as it was delivering food at par with New York /London /Paris. The Bar at F9 became famous with our innovative flare bartenders, and stylish cocktails.

F9 soon became a destination for not only the expats, but also for everyone. Now Hyderabad had a place where they could bring anyone for both wining and dining, and within three month's time, the *Times Of India* declared their poll results, awarding the best restaurant overall title to F9 in terms of food, service, ambience, as well as experience.

Hyderabad had finally arrived on the international food map. There was a lot of coverage over the years in various national magazines, and television with the expats and IT professionals, listing us in their favourite and must visit places. I could feel the change and felt wonderful. When I was on the plane from Dubai back to Hyderabad, I came across a group of five ladies from HSBC bank transferred from London to Hyderabad. They were talking about the brief given to them in London, and the main dining option was F9. All these people were staying in five-star hotels. It was indeed a proud moment for me and I was happy with the turnaround on food the city was witnessing.

Meanwhile the traditional restaurants in Hyderabad still continue to boom, but F9 became a benchmark for any new place opening up. Five years down the line, *Times* has yet again awarded F9 as the best restaurant in the overall category. Buoyed by the confidence instilled in me, I started working on a new concept of South East Asian restaurant right above F9. It was the first Teppanyaki restaurant in Hyderabad city. The new style decor, and ambience was an instant hit and the way Japanese, Thai, Vietnamese food moved, showed how aware the people had become. The Hyderabadis were ready to experiment with the right presentation, and good quality food, offering the right kind of response. Hyderabad was maturing beautifully.

The next restaurant I started was Deli9, the first true Delhi food joint. Hyderabad always had a sweet tooth, and F9 was the first restaurant to do without Indian desserts, as we did only global desserts.

One of the greatest indicators of the changing tastes of the city was when I hosted a 'Dessert Festival' in F9 for ten days. There was on offing global desserts together with Indian desserts by Almond House (one of the best and most successful sweet shop in Hyderabad). Surprisingly, the offtake was 95 percent global desserts, 5 percent Indian desserts. This was three years back. I went about asking people the reason for this sea change, and the stock answer was that the time for change has come and the awareness of global cuisine is high.

One of my fondest memories is of the times when my regular visitors used to comment on the fact that the food tasted the same or better. It was a great encouragement to all of us to do better. F9 was also exciting for everyone because I changed menus every three month. There is still to date a 75 percent loyalty clientele, and a changing dynamic new lot too.

Five years has passed now, and Hyderabad has taken a huge leap towards modernisation on all fronts. Today the city is peppered with a variety of cuisines. New hotels are rising and many more are on the horizon. All world class brands, great food and beverages, are in the offing and great times are ahead. Yet the delicious biryani still booms in popularity, right up there. All this shows that the city is moving in the right direction, yet still retaining the old favourites.

How real is real estate?

I. Syam Prasad Reddy

Real estate and infrastructure are the hottest sectors in India today. The sector is booming with many players stepping into this field. It has also begun to have an impact on several other businesses in the economy with billions of dollars being poured in.

In the last three years, property prices have shot up by 150-200 percent in all metros, crossing even the peak prices of 1990s when a property boom enveloped the nation. This time the wave of optimism has also spread to smaller cities where prices are spiraling to unimaginable limits.

A recent study by the Associated Chambers of Commerce and Industry of India (ASSOCHAM) says that India's real estate market will expand from Rs 70,400 crore to Rs 264,000 crore by 2010. This boom is attracting several excited overseas investors who are estimated to pump in Rs 110,000 crore into the industry.

But it hasn't always been like this in the city of Nizams that was once a land of lakes, rocks, wilderness and jungles. In Banjara

Hills, which is a prime locality now, we could find wild boars and peacocks bang in the middle of the road. Though several lament over the loss of landscape, I feel this is a by-product of growth. There is no question of looking back. If there is any way to look at, it is ahead. If there is one way this can go it is up. 'Up and Ahead' is the modern day mantra for the city that is zooming on the growth graph.

Boom in Hyderabad

With real estate prices in many of the metros skyrocketing, investors are now on the look out for cities where the amenities for setting up base are conducive. Hyderabad has emerged as one of the hottest destination of choice for many investors.

The Andhra Pradesh government has been promoting IT/ITeS growth in the city and has launched significant incentives for companies setting up offices in the state. These include the status of 'essential services' provided to the IT/ITeS sector and 100 percent reimbursement on stamp duty.

With real estate being available around Hyderabad, space to set up infrastructure is not a problem. Besides, about 350,000 graduates from universities across the state are available, ensuring a steady supply of the required human resource.

The demand and a healthy supply of 'raw material' have encouraged developers to plan and announce major projects in the city. Areas like Kukatpally, Madhapur, Gachibowli have proved to be a happy hunting ground for these developers because of their close proximity to the Hi-Tech city and availability of land among other reasons. In the last year itself, Hyderabad saw a supply of 6.2 million sq. ft of land, of which 3.4 million sq. ft was pre-committed.

The planned supply in the next 5-8 quarters is in excess of 20 million sq ft of which Indu alone would develop 2 million sq.ft. Most leading developers have aggressive plans to tap this commercial market. This in turn has increased the need for residential spaces. The above-mentioned areas have seen a sharp rise in the construction of residential spaces. Apartments, housing complexes and integrated townships providing all amenities are coming up in a big way. However, this has not touched the rentals. The rate of rentals has remained static and stable.

A name to reckon with

When we entered the scene, Hyderabad was seen as a promising city in terms of real estate but nobody could predict the unprecedented boom. Our now famous townships in the city were considered to be outskirts then. Though we began our tryst with Hyderabad as a real estate and construction company, it didn't take long for us to diversify into related fields. Today, Indu Group is an end-to-end solutions provider in Infrastructure and Real Estate industry, based in Hyderabad, India with operations spread across the country. We have world-class expertise in developing IT parks, IT SEZ, residential townships, shopping malls, multiplexes, hotels, theme ventures, as well as core infrastructure like irrigation projects and roads.

Our multidisciplinary capabilities and specialisation ranging from design, construction management to whole-life asset management helps us offer our customers complete end-to-end solutions. When we began providing such an array of services, many people asked us: 'Where are the takers?' Today, we have customers booking their units with us in the first few weeks of the launch itself. Now everybody is saying 'you were in the right place at the right time'.

There can't be a city better for our business than Hyderabad today. With all the advantages of a modern, well-developed city, this is probably the only destination in India where old world charm still rules. The per capita income has risen phenomenally but cost of living is still very affordable. Not surprisingly, the standard of living of average residents has improved tremendously.

What differentiates Indu Group from the rest is improved efficiency, enhanced effectiveness, greater flexibility and adaptability. To offer total value for their investment, we offer our customers the complete value chain in the capacity of a Realtor, Developer, Builder and an end-to-end Solutions Provider.

I started Indu Projects in December 2001. That wasn't too long ago but for a city that is on an accelerated growth mode, it seems like an eternity. Much water has flown since then and we have grown by leaps and bounds taking our investors far beyond their imaginations and ours. The journey though enduring hasn't really been a cakewalk.

When we began promoting our first residential township in Kukatpally, bang next to an industrial area, buyers were skeptical. We had to convince them that it was one of its kind. But now it's the turn of our buyers to queue up for our townships. So what, it's the same all over the country, one might argue. I, however, beg to differ. You must understand first and foremost that a Hyderabadi is like none other when it comes to putting his money. He is extremely conservative when it comes to his investments. Not for him the quick buck schemes or in the future you'll be a billionaire dreams. What he wants is hard core value for his money which in a way is good because then they don't easily fall prey to scams.

It was my dream that Indu's foundation be based on research and not just on the growth drive, as is prevalent in the industry. As this idea grew stronger, I hoped that it would be beneficial to the industry as a whole. This prompted me to initiate a tie-up between Indu Group and the Indian School of Business at Hyderabad to institute a Research Chair in Real Estate & Infrastructure.

I would like to take a bow to this city, which has made my mission possible, and my dream a reality. And I think this is just the beginning. *Salaam* Hyderabad.

All things Hyderabadi

Vanaja Banagiri

History

When a poet, architect and an artist supervises the building of a city, beauty, balance and proportion are to be expected. What lends an air of romance to the city of Hyderabad, is the love story of a young prince and a village belle that resulted in its birth.

There is a love story related to the founding of the city of Hyderabad. As a young prince, Muhammad Quli fell passionately in love with a maiden from Chichlam village across the river Musi. He would even venture to cross the river to meet his beloved. Ibrahim Qutb Shah, his father, built a bridge on the river so that the crown prince did not endanger his life in this infatuation. When he ascended the throne, Muhammad Quli built a grand structure, the Charminar, at the site of the village. The city was called Bhagyanagar to appease his beloved, Bhagmati. Later on it came to be called Hyderabad. Bhagyanagar means the 'city of good fortune'.

The history of Hyderabad begins with the establishment of the Qutub Shahi dynasty. Quli Qutub Shah seized the reins of power from the Bahamani Kingdom in 1512 and established the fortress city of Golconda. Inadequacy of water, and frequent epidemics of plague and cholera forced Mohammed, the fifth Quli Qutub Shahi ruler to venture outward to establish the new city Hyderabad, with the Charminar at its centre and with four great roads fanning out in the four cardinal directions.

Culture

The Muslim culture of Hyderabad refers to the culture associated with Muslims of the erstwhile Hyderabad State. With its origins in the Muslim Bahmani Sultanate and then Deccan sultanates, the culture became defined in the latter half of the reign of the Asif Jahi dynasty in Hyderabad. The culture exists today in Hyderabad and among the Hyderabadi Muslim diaspora around the world, in particular, Pakistan, Saudi Arabia, the Arab states of the Persian Gulf, USA, Canada and the United Kingdom. The Deccan plateau acted as a bulwark sheltering South India from the invasions and political turmoil that affected North India. This allowed the Muslim-ruled state of Hyderabad to develop a distinctive culture during the Qutb Shahi dynasty and later the Asaf Jahi dynasty of the Nizams.

The seventh Nizam, Osman Ali Pasha, was the richest man in the world in his period.

The Nizam was the Muslim ruler of the vast princely Hyderabad State. The capital city of Hyderabad was primarily Urdu-speaking Muslim until the Independence of India and subsequent rise to dominance of Telugu-speaking people of Andhra. The state's economy was agrarian, and Hyderabad was primarily a government and administrative hub, run mostly (but far from exclusively) by Muslims. The aristocracy, *jagirdars* and

Osman Ali Pasha

deshmukhs (wealthy landowners), and even minor government officials could afford to hire servants, usually also Muslims, in a social order similar to the class system of Victorian England. The Nizam allied himself with the British early on, with ensuing political stability. The Muslim upper and middle classes were left free to concentrate on a carefree and leisurely lifestyle involving clothes, jewellery, food, music, literary arts, and other indulgences, little of which trickled down to the servant class, known as *naukar* (a word originally used for the Mughal Emperor Babur's closest feudal retainers).

The relative isolation of Hyderabad until Independence, its distinctive dialect of Urdu and the strong web of interconnecting family relationships that characterises Hyderabadi Muslims sometimes leads to charges of parochialism from other Indian Muslim communities, but it also ensures a Hyderabadi Muslim identity endures among the Indian diaspora.

Language and Literature

One of the most identifiable markers of Hyderabadi Muslim culture is the local dialect of Urdu known as Dakhni. There is a lighthearted saying that Urdu was born in Lukhnow, murdered in Hyderabad and buried in Bangalore! Dakhni is distinct due to its mixture of vocabulary from Marathi and Telugu, as well as some vocabulary from Arabic, Persian and Turkish that are not found in the standard dialect of Urdu. In terms of pronunciation, the easiest way to recognise a Hyderabadi Muslim is their pronunciation of letter 'qāf' (ق) as 'kh' (خ). The most distinctive aspect about the city of Hyderabad is the fact that the local Hindu population also speaks Hyderabadi Urdu as their native language unlike their counterparts in the rest of the state regions of Andhra Pradesh (Andhra and Rayalseema) who speak Telugu.

Certain words are very typical of Hyderabadis:

Nakko (instead of *Nahi* in Traditional Urdu) =No
Hau (instead of *Han* in Traditional Urdu) =Yes
Kaiku (instead of *Kyun* in Traditional Urdu) =Why

Mereku (instead of *Mujhe* in Traditional Urdu) = For me
Tereku (instead of *Tujhe* in Traditional Urdu) =For you
Mye (instead of *Mai* in Traditional Urdu) =Me

These are some examples of liaisons that are peculiar only to Hyderabadi Urdu:

Jatiyun (Jaati Hoon) = I'm going (female)
Aatiyun (Aati Hoon) = I'm coming (female)
Kartiyun (Karti Hoon) = Will do (female)
Bolinge (Bolangay) = They will say
Karlinge (Karlangay) = We will do it
Bheto (Bhaytoh) = Sit (Please Sit)
Jainge (Jayangay) = We will go
Aainge (Aayangay) = We will come
Thairinge (Theheraingay) = We will stay

Cuisine and Hospitality

The 400 years of Hyderabadi culture has its origin in art, music, dance, poetry and jewellery, but the most popular is its cuisine. Hyderabad is never complete without the mention of the *Shahi Dastarkhan*. The *Dastarkhan* is the dining place where the food is served and eaten. It is normally a low chowki for the dining table and cotton mattresses for squatting and bolsters for the back rest. The *Dastarkhan* holds a place of reverence in every household.

What makes the Hyderabadi cuisine special is the use of special ingredients, carefully chosen and cooked to the right degree. The addition of a certain herb, spice, condiment, or an amalgam of these adds a unique taste and texture. The herbs and spices used and the method of preparation gives the dish its unique name. *Murgh do pyaza* gets its name from the onions that are added twice to the dish in two variations. The *masalas* or the rich blend of herbs, spices and condiments give the dishes a base, or what is popularly known as 'gravy'. Some of these blends are a well-kept secret that passes only down the family line or from the Ustad (Teacher) to his Shagird (Pupil). The head cooks or the *Khansamas* were an asset to the household, and were treated with due respect.

The word 'Nawabi' is as synonymous with the Hyderabadi cuisine as 'Shahi' is with Luknowi. These terms conjure delicacies that are rich in taste and texture with mouth-watering aromas. The *Kebabs* in Hyderabad need a special mention; the *Shammi Kebab* is one such popular dish. Hard to believe that the *Kebabs* were originally from Greece! The Hyderabadi meal is never complete without the bread from the kilns of the local bakers. The breads from this cuisine are equally popular, be it rich *Sheermal* or *lukmi* (bread stuffed with savory mince meat). Bread is not only an accompaniment to the meal but forms a base for a popular sweet dish *Double Ka Meetha*.

Hyderabad's strong Mughlai influence is perhaps the reason why the Hyderabadi Biryani has become so popular all over India. This famous dish has been experimented time and again to perfection. In fact the Biryani has influenced a Hyderabadi's tongue so strongly that usually other famous dishes of Hyderabad takes a back seat. It take an extra ordinary taste for other dishes to beat the competition of Biryani.

Some other famous Hyderabadi dishes that are served at weddings are: *Haleem, Khubani ka Mitha, Gil-e-Firdaus, Double Ka Meetha, Luqmi, Dum ka qimah, Muthhi Key Kebabs, Mirchi ka Salan* and *Baghare Baigan*.

Other popular food items are: *Chakna, Tamate ka Kut, Khatti Dal, Dalcha, Shirmal, Rawghani Roti, Nihari, Pasande, Pathar Ka Ghosht, Dum Ka Murgh,Khagina, Katchi Biryani, Khichri* and *Qabuli.*

Many Hyderabadi dishes are very sour because of the generous use of tamarind. As a result, Hyderabadis are sometimes jokingly called *khatte* ('sour' in Urdu). Interestingly, many old time hakeems believed that tamarind besides being an aphrodisiac also heightened the libido and the sperm count. That theory probably explains the countless children the nawabs and nizams sired.

Clothing and Jewellery

Hyderabad is famous for its pearl *bazaar*. Pearls from all over the world are said to come to Hyderabad because the artisans here are skilled in piercing and stringing pearls without damaging them. The city's gypsy tribes called Lambadas and Banjaras are known throughout India for their colourful costumes.

A Khara Dupatta and hyderabadi jewellery are traditionally worn by a Hyderabadi bride.

The *Khara Dupatta* (standing veil) is an outfit composed of a *kurta* (tunic), *chooridaar* (ruched pair of pants), and six-yard *dupatta* (veil) and is traditionally worn by Hyderabadi brides. Sometimes the *kurta* is sleeveless and worn over a *koti* resembling a choli. The bride also wears a matching *ghoonghat* (veil) over her head. The accompanying jewellery is:

- *Tika* (a medallion of uncut diamonds worn on the forehead and suspended by a string of pearls)
- *Jhoomar* (a fan shaped ornament worn on the side of the head)
- *Nath* (a nose ring with a large ruby bead flanked by two pearls)
- *Chintaak* (a choker studded with uncut diamonds and precious stones)
- *Karan phool* (earrings that match the *Chintaak* and consist of a flower motif covering the ear lobe and a bell shaped ornament that is suspended from the flower. The

weight of precious stones and gold in the *Karan phool* is held up by *sahare* or supports made of strands of pearls that are fastened into the wearers hair.)

- *Satlada* (neck ornament of seven strands of pearls set with emeralds, diamonds and rubies)
- *Ranihaar* (neck ornament of pearls with a wide pendant)
- *Jugni* (neck ornament of several strands of pearls with a central pendant)
- *Goat* (Shellac bangles studded with rhinestones and worn with gold colored glass bangles called *sonabai*)
- *Payal* (ankle bracelets)
- *Gintiyan* (toe rings)

Hyderabadi Gentleman and the Sherwani

The Sherwani is the traditional men's garb of Hyderabad. It is a coat-like tunic with a tight-fitting collar (fastened with hooks), close-fitting in the upper torso and flaring somewhat in its lower half. It usually has six or seven buttons, often removable ones made from gold sovereigns for special occasions. The material is usually silk or wool. A groom may use gold brocade for his wedding sherwani, but otherwise good taste dictates understated colors, albeit with rich and textured fabrics. The sherwani is usually worn over a silk or cotton *kurta* (long shirt) and *pyjamas* (baggy pants with a drawstring at the waist).

The sherwani is closely associated with Hyderabad, although it has spread since to the rest of India and to Pakistan. Prime Minister Jawaharlal Nehru adapted its design and turned it into his trademark Nehru Jacket, further popularising the garment.

Religion

Hyderabad has both Sunni and Shi'ah Muslims, the majority of them being Sunni .The Sunni Muslims mostly follow the Hanafi school of Islamic Jurisprudence, although there are a few who follow the Shafi'i school of thought and mainly reside in areas close to Barkas, the former Military Barracks of the Nizam, an area where the residents are mainly of a Yemeni descent (especially from Hadhramawt). The Deobandi Tablighi Jamaat is also active. Salafism is slowly becoming popular with educated youth due to its appeal as a purer form of Islam than the local popular custom. The political Jamaat-e-Islami is also visible in the Mehdipatnam region where its large main mosque, Masjid e Azizia, is located.

Religious knowledge and its propagation flourished under the Nizam with institutions like the world famous Jamia Nizamia (Jami'ah Nizamiyyah) of Hyderabad. The largest Mosque of Hyderabad, the Makkah Masjid gathers congregations of two hundred thousand and more on special occasions of Eid prayers and especially of Jumu'at-al Wida' (the last Friday of Ramadan known as Ramzan in Hyderabad)

Changing attitudes

Evolution has found a new destination—Hyderabad. Or should that be revolution? Any which way you look at it, whatever term you wish to use to describe the winds of change that have swept the city, one thing is certain. Hyderabad has arrived. And how!

Gone are the days of *nawabi* attitudes and laid back life styles. Everything is on a fast track. From economic development to attitudinal change, Hyderabad has undergone a tremendous metomorphosis. Steering the growth are the city's young. With their restlessness to be a part of the hip and happening and energy levels to match, they have redefined all things hitherto known as Hyderabadi.

Shopping, clubbing or weddings, every single opportunity is an event to be celebrated. And that too, in a larger than life way. A twenty-something doesn't bat an eyelid before she picks up a pair of Jimmy Choo shoes or a Prada bag. And the big fat middle-aged Hyderabadi has turned into six-pack exhibitionist strutting his stuff. Male manicures are a daily norm and tequila shots are nightly rituals. While the rest of the country parties on weekends, Hyderabadis do it everyday. Eves nights at night clubs and pubs are jam-packed with the young and the not so old, while the fuddy-duddies are having a whale of a time in their Jubilee hills, Banjara hills mansions.

Changing landscape

Another aspect that has undergone a tremendous change is the look of buildings with so many offshore companies setting up shop in the City's HITEC City, the IT Mecca. Anybody who drives through the area can't believe they are in erstwhile Hyderabad. You could be in Singapore, Malaysia or even US. The city's architectural landscape has opened the eyes of many non-Hyderabadis. Even homes look different now. Till recently, Hyderabadis couldn't relate to apartment culture. After much resistance, they have succumbed to the housing demands and escalating land rates and one can find high rises mushrooming in and around the city. Fortunately, some areas like the Jubilee Hills are protected from the onslaught of modern day wonders and still retain the charm of homes with gardens.

Hyderabadis are all over the place now, almost everywhere in the world across continents, countries, prairies, deserts, great lakes, green forests, islands. Everywhere. The Hyderabadi diaspora continues to expand just as the city stretches from

Shamshabad to Shamirpet today. A long way from where it started. But, as we here never tire of reminding the rest of the world and ourselves—once a Hyderabadi, always a Hyderabadi. So they keep coming back to find old haunts gone, buildings pulled down and turned into malls and multiplexes, homes razed and converted into three-hundred and fifty flats on five hundred yards and being sold at exorbitant rates. Well, well, times—they are changing fast.

The Hyderabadi trademark

So what has remained unchanged? The warmth of the soul, the hospitality, the tendency to trust and good old Hyderabadi Urdu. *Kaiku* hasn't become *kyun* and *nakko* hasn't changed to *nahin*. And yes, *parson* still ranges from one week to several years but never day before yesterday or day after tomorrow. Like they say, you can take a Hyderabadi out of Hyderabad but not Hyderabad out of a Hyderabadi. Says Imtiyaz, a businessman: 'Recently at an immigration queue in Heathrow there were two suited, booted gentlemen accompanied by women in short skirts with streaked hair. I passed them of as angrez from the way they looked. Their complexions, English accent et al. Until one of them, impatient with the delay, burst out, '*Kithi der lagarein ji in logan. India say kharab hai*.'(How long are these guys taking? It's worse than India). Nothing like chaste Hyderabadi to de-stress. Only a Hyderabadi can relate to that.

Hyderabad Hazir Hai is a tribute to the Hyderabadi spirit that remains untouched over the generations. Eighteen authors and one book...as diverse as only this city of minarets can be. Say *Amen*, *Tathastu* or *Aadab*. We respond in one language, the language of unity and in one sentence—*hum logaan aisich hai*. (We are like this only.)

Once Upon a Time

Vijay Marur

Once upon a time I was a child wearing fashionably airy shorts and cycling to the quaintest corners of the city without worrying about anything but the kandeel (small kerosene lamp) that was a statutory requirement.

Once upon a time is a memory. When understandably bored with Granny's tales at home, we would explore the bylanes of the city, hoping to bump into some interesting storytellers. And find them in the strangest of places. At Irani cafes, bus stops, kabab joints, barbershop. Even while sitting in a cycle-rickshaw.

Here are a few stories. Tales that have been recounted to me by people whose faces I have forgotten. But the stories themselves remain deeply imprinted on my mind. In all fairness I must confess that it is stories like these that not only helped me understand the Hyderabadi psyche, but also contributed significantly to my evolution into someone who is proud to call Hyderabad his home. And most of all helped me understand that a true Hyderabadi never lies. He merely embellishes the truth.

The Hakeem and his Daughter

Beyond Charminar is a world called Shalibanda (Shah-Ali-Banda). You can recognise it by the sound of industrious hands beating gold into a wafer thin leaf that can be used to clad everything from temple domes to minaret crowns. You can recognise it by the plethora of colourfully graphic boards that invite you to get your broken bones set.

It was while hanging around the periphery of Shalibanda, sipping a sweet lassi, that I was first told about the fact that this was possibly the last remaining bastion of Nafas (or Nafs), the pulse diagnostic discipline of the Unani School of Medicine.

Nafas is an ancient Ayurvedic and Unani diagnostic technique that's based on the reading of the pulse. And here in this lane apparently lived a doctor, a Hakeem, who was a Nafas specialist. His practice was booming they told me as they recounted several miraculous stories of diagnosis and healing. But the one that in present day parlance, blew my mind, was the one about the Hakeem and his daughter.

Apparently the Hakeem's daughter, being a product of the new generation used to pooh-pooh the claims of her father's science. And was convinced that her father's popularity was driven by a bit of medicinally coated skullduggery and a great amount of good luck. So she decided to test her father. The next day, in connivance with a few friends, she bunked school, put on her burkha (veil) and stood in line outside the clinic like an ordinary patient, waiting for the Hakeem Sahib to arrive.

When it was her turn to consult with the doctor she extended her hand to the assistant who tied a string to her wrist and gave its other end from behind the screen to the great man. This was done because in those days the strict rules of *purdah* demanded that not only should strangers not see a woman's face, they should also not be allowed to touch her.

Expecting the doctor to deliver a diagnosis that had to be wrong or hilarious or both, the girl was shocked out of her wits when the Hakeem, after just holding the string for a fraction of a second, reprimanded her in a paternally stern tone: 'Daughter, aren't you supposed to be at school today?'

Dara Singh and King Kong

Indian freestyle wrestling was a great favourite of the crowds. Every year hoardings would be put up announcing matches between giants like Dara Singh, Flash Gordon, Randhawa and King Kong. Those of us who were not fortunate enough to witness the matches live had to depend on the post match commentary that we could tune in to at any café near Nampally. Typically there would be a pehelwan (wrestler) of sorts who would set up court at a corner table. His chamchas (sidekicks if you didn't know) would order endless numbers of *chai* and between crisp bites of the Osmania biscuits and slurpy swallows of tea from the saucer, the man would launch into a blow-by-blow account of the match.

And this is where the story becomes interesting. Dara Singh for instance was supposedly about eight feet tall. And weighed just under 200 kg. King Kong, the champion from Hong Kong was a good two feet taller and tipped the scales after the two quintal mark. (Please note the 100 percent mark up that's peculiar to the Hyderabadi School of Storytelling). The fight began in a terribly one sided manner. King Kong was throwing Dara Singh around as if he was but a rag doll. A couple of times it looked like the fight was over. A battered Dara Singh was about to throw in the towel. And then, depending on who was telling the story or who was obviously listening to it, a little boy cried or a pretty young woman cried, 'Come on Dara Singh!'

And Dara Singh came back to life. Came back into the fight with a thump, a thwack and a thadam! His famous aeroplane swing came into play and having picked up King Kong like a sack of potatoes, Dara Singh flung him across the forty feet broad ring, across the first few rows of audience. King Kong the mighty lay vanquished, unconscious, defeated.

Dara Singh had won. Again.

The story was full of inconsistencies, full of multiplication factors that took it beyond the realms of the unbelievable. But what took the cake was the answer that was provided when someone in the audience, almost on cue, asked what the secret of Dara Singh's strength was. Two dozen boiled eggs, six whole chickens, twelve glasses of milk, twenty *aloo paranthas* and a few *seers* of pure *desi ghee*. That is what Dara Singh eats everyday for breakfast, the storyteller would announce with awe. And when asked how he knew such intimate details about the Champion's eating regimen, he would smirk, he would shrug and announce almost shyly that he knew, because he was there with the wrestler at breakfast time. We would all head back home thinking Dara Singh was India's answer to Superman. And eat a slightly heavier dinner than usual much to our parents' concern. And in our sleep we would throw pillows around after pummeling them into meek submission.

The next days' newspaper would wake us up with a headline that announced with great regret that due to unavoidable circumstances, Dara Singh hadn't made it to the Wrestling Championships at Hyderabad that year. The report would go on to say that Dara Singh who was now recuperating in Punjab, had promised to be there for next years' championships. Definitely.

As I grew up on this staple diet of stories that were replete with unimaginable twists, unabashed exaggeration and an unmistakable flair for drama, I came to believe that the city had surely reached the limits of its own gullibility. But the next two stories will show you how utterly wrong I was.

The day the Tank Bund burst

For a while, we lived in an area called Domalguda. Literally translated the name means 'the abode of the mosquitoes' and if you have lived there you'll agree that the locality does indeed live up to its name.

Domalguda is a low lying area. A colony that came up in the lowlands of the Hussain Sagar lake, it had an eclectic mix of huts and 'pucca construction' houses. We were fortunately in a bungalow that had a nice big terrace. Our neighbourhood however was a smattering of huts. Given that most of the people who lived in those huts had spouses or children who worked for us in several capacities, I used to call them our Servants' Quarters.

One evening, while I was waiting for the familiar sound of my father's StationWagon I heard an ominous rumble. I looked around but before I could identify the source, a crowd of hysterically screaming hut dwellers barged into our house. And since most of them were familiar with the layout, they ran up the stairs to the terrace before I had a chance to either object or to ask them about their motives.

My father arrived shortly thereafter and was understandably quite upset that I had let in half the city's destitutes into our house. When he said, 'We'll thrash this out later' it didn't take too much intelligence to figure out what was in store for me. With my mother in tow, we climbed up the stairs to the terrace where we were greeted by loud howls of despair and cries of agony.

'We are finished sir. We are doomed madam. Only you can save us now,' the voices said. Except that we had to rely on a keen sense of translation to decipher the incoherent garble that was actually emanating from those harrowed countenances. When my father calmed them down and asked them what the problem was, the funniest story emerged.

'The Tank Bund has burst,' someone had told them. The zillions of gallons of water that the lake was made up of had burst the seam and tidal waves were inundating the city, washing off whatever came in their way. Several hutments had vanished. Children had been sucked into raging whirlpools. Families were missing. But thank God they lived next to a bungalow. Next to a solid construction which they were sure would be able to bear the onslaught of whatever waves Hussain Sagar generated in its breach.

That's when we realised that each family had carried with them not just the little children, the stray puppies, the utensils, the rickety kerosene stoves and so on, but also trunks and half broken wooden chests that contained almost everything they owned.

My father slipped authoritatively into his man of science, man of logic mode. And tried to reason with them. He tried to tell them that if the Bund had indeed burst, there was not enough water in the lake to wash away an entire colony, leave alone the city. He tried to tell them that even if he was wrong about his calculations, what was undeniable was the fact that too much time had passed and that whatever they feared would happen, should already have happened. But to no avail. We were dealing with a mob whose primal instincts of survival had been triggered. And it looked like we would have to bear with their company till morning dawned or better sense prevailed, whichever was earlier.

Just as I was wondering whether our roof was strong enough to support all these people, I saw something that as the story goes, saved the day. From the rooftop I spotted the comforting sight of brightly lit double-decker buses going peacefully across the Tank Bund.

The view from the top had never looked better. And faced with irrefutable evidence that the Tank Bund was intact, the crowd slowly shuffled off towards their respective huts. Leaving behind in their wake one cyclone affected house, one hurricane impacted family and one fat little kid whose respect for the Hyderabadi art of storytelling had just gone up several notches.

Who told them that the Bund had burst? No one knows. Who spread the rumour? No one knows. But I am sure that somewhere there's a man or a woman who hasn't been able to wipe the smile of sadistic satisfaction off his or her face. After all the objective of storytelling, and indeed the measure of credibility, is to move your listeners. And that had surely been achieved.

The Blood Sucking Old Lady

Getting a cycle rickshaw walla to take you to your destination was an art. There were times when cajoling worked. Sometimes you had to be tough. Sometimes you had to play the exhausted, helpless passenger with panache. If all this failed, you had to jingle some extra music of the monetary kind. But when the last lap of your journey was a slope that you knew he would have to struggle up, you often had to resort to delivering truth in installments.

So one day when I was too tired to walk back from a friend's place in Somajiguda and I wanted to hire a rickshaw to pedal me up to our house in Banjara Hills, I got on confidently onto the back and said, 'Take me to Punjagutta'.

Sitting in a Hyderabadi rickshaw was a unique experience. The distance between the floor and the seat was so little that you willy-nilly had to sit in the lotus position, which at the best of times, was not my favourite yogic torture. But with the ulterior motive of tricking him up the slope I grinned and struck up a conversation with him.

Did he have kids? Were they going to school? Did he want them to become rickshaw wallas when they grew up? You get the drift. And obviously it worked, because when we reached Punjagutta and I very casually asked him to turn left, he did so without even the semblance of a grumble. We had gone but a few yards and just as I was getting ready to deliver the next instalment of truth—that he had to pedal up the slope—the man suddenly brought the rickshaw to a sudden stop. He turned around to look at me. And I, who was expecting anything from irritation to disdain, was shocked when I saw written large on his face, the unmistakable stench of fear.

'I will not take you up this road,' he stuttered.

'But why?' I asked. Mentally prepared to walk the rest of the way, but still cursing my luck. What kind of a nutcase chicken had I found?

'You don't know?' He asked, his voice a stammer in the dark.

'Know what?' I asked with the right tone of incredulity.

'Up this lane lives the Blood Sucker Lady!' he croaked.

He then told me a story that curdled many a walk up that lane. Apparently in one of the houses up the road, there lived a woman. She was from noble stock and lived in a fair amount of comfort. Everything about her was fine except that she had a strange desire to stay young forever. And some tantric had given her the power to realise her dreams. All she needed was a daily dose of young male blood. Every evening she would lurk around the darkening corners and grab the first young man she saw, dragging him into her house. Suffice to say that while nobody knew what she did inside to the hapless young man, he would emerge a few hours later. Entirely drained. Sapped. And aged. And she could be seen flush with renewed youth, rejuvenated in body, mind and soul.

'It's that time of the evening now,' mumbled my charioteer. 'And there is no way I am going to cycle up the lane,' he added. And without even taking the proffered 50 paise for the half ride, he disgorged me unceremoniously and pedaled away furiously towards the safer side of the city.

Now I was in a fix. Should I walk up the hill? Or not. Should I stick to the left side? Or to the right. Should I run? Should I wait for someone else and walk along as a group? Questions like these echoed in my mind for some time. I then decided to be brave. And recalled the mantra Grandma had taught us when we were kids. I closed my eyes—prayed, chanted under my breath, and meditated. When I opened my eyes, I was in front of my gate—at home and safe.

So four little stories from my memory banks; stories that I heard; stories that I lived. Sure. More importantly, stories that have but one message. That once upon a time in Hyderabad, there used to live a phenomenon called exaggeration who had a friend called approximation. And guess what, they still live here happily ever after.

Hyderabadi Adventure

Vinita Pittie

Life in Hyderabad has given me more than I could ask for, in a lifetime. Armed with a legacy of discipline, punctuality and hard work from my parents, I found a comfortable cushy balance at my marital home in Hyderabad which relieved me of any kind of stress and put me in a comfort zone. Though a housewife at heart I run a designing enterprise that allows me to translate my dreams into reality. Life is hectic but nevertheless quite satisfying.

Let me begin from my introduction to Hyderabad. As a new entrant into the quaint Hyderabad culture, I would never have imagined that all of whatever is uttered is not meant literally (Thumb rule No.1).

Once we drove through the crooked lanes and halted at a dead end. '*Gaadi palta lo,*' shouted the policeman. '*Seedha jao, chadhav pay chado, utaar pay utaro!*' What funny directions! My young mind imagined us driving in an upside down car. (I had heard of only upside down pudding before!) We turned around and retraced our way. A new lingo that I was sure to learn by and by.

At home the usherer announced, '*Kaunki ladies aaye.*' No, there weren't ten of them. Not five, not even two—just one lady but why use singular when you can use plural. That's Hyderabadi logic for you. Funnier still, at my brief meeting with the 'ladies', she told me about the river Musi which had flooded parson (day after). I had not been apprised of the eternal quality of the everlasting time-embodying term.

The salesman and the jeweller; the tailor and the carpenter; the electrician and the plumber—all of them promised to deliver parson. You would have heard 'tomorrow never comes'. But who could have thought of the day after the day that never comes! Blissful existence! Or Hyderabadi attitude?

Hyderabad—a melting pot of cultures? Nah! A boiling pot of cultures I would say. You might run head on into a camel on the road though there are other creatures, too. The choice is yours—cows, bulls, buffaloes, hens, dogs, cats.... No, we're not passing by a farmland, we just crossed the greenlands and have stopped at a railway crossing. The guard promises that the train will arrive in '*paanch dus...pandrah minute...aadha ghanta*'. Meanwhile *aap ke paas* tollywood-bollywood music *hai ich* to hear. Or else read a book.

My romantic adventure had begun. Perhaps one day, I would write my own book on the 'Discovery of Hyderabad'. The messenger who left two hours ago has not arrived so far. He didn't fall asleep. He simply forgot! *Bhool ich gaya*! Today, the amnesia had been cured; slumber evades us; there is intense activity; our booming presence on the global map has led us to the famed Golconda diamonds at the end of the rainbow.

We are young as we are old; sleepy yet alert; *noveau riche* and aristocratically rich. The beggars carry mobiles; the roadside salons offer 'Hairdressing and Setting with Dryer also'. The canteen and Irani hotel have 'meals are ready' always. There are Ramazan and Diwali discount sales throughout the year. And as we party everyday Quli Qutb Shah's Hyderabad remains blessed with his wish that his island be so full of people like the sea with fish! *Aameen*! So be it and so it is. Yes, *huzoor 'parson* has arrived' like it does only in Hyderabad.

Know More About Our Contributors

Ali Zahir (b.1947) is a well known Urdu writer from Hyderabad. He lived in Iran from 1974-1980 which brought him closer to the Persian Literary Sources. He also lived through the trauma of the Iranian Revolution of 1979. He has published five collection of verses and two books of critical essays. A collection of his English poems was published from England in 1991 under the title *Seven Days Seven Heavens*. Not only that, he has written scripts for TV serials and plays and made some documentary films in English.

At present he is Consultant to the National Council for the Promotion of Urdu Language Southern Region (HRD Ministry).

❖

Aminuddin Khan was born in Hyderabad in 1932. Scion of an old noble family of the former princely State, he was educated at the Doon School, Dehra Dun, and Nizam College, Hyderabad. He then spent sixteen years in the South Indian hills, tea planting and studying the wildlife and biography of the region. He is also the author of *A Right Royal Bastard* published by Rupa & Co.

Bakhtiar K. Dadabhoy, is a civil servant based in Secunderabad. He was educated at Hindu College, Delhi University, and at the Delhi School of Economics. He is the author of five books including *A Dictionary of Dates*, the bestselling *Jeh: A Life of JRD Tata* and more recently *Sugar in Milk: Lives of Eminent Parsis*. He is also the author of two books on cricket, a game of which despite match-fixing he remains a great fan.

❖

Dinaz Noria was born in 1963 in Mumbai, Maharashtra. After a short career as cabin crew with British Airways, she moved to Hyderabad and forayed into store front displays and visual merchandising. She experienced a natural progression into set design for theatre, fashion shows, corporate dos and weddings. Currently she runs 3-D, a decor design company based in Hyderabad with operations in Chennai and Bangalore she lives in Hyderabad with husband Gusti Noria and son Kynan, who is the sunshine of her life.

❖

Born in 1962 in a poet's family in India, **Fawad Tamkanat** acquired a Master's Degree in Fine Arts after graduating in Commerce. He is the recipients of the University Gold Medals in BFA and MFA, Central University, Hyderabad, India.

Fawad Tamkanat's works are in display in the collection of National Gallery of Modern Art, New Delhi; Vingsted Center, Denmark; Lalit Kala Academy, besides many public and private collections in India and abroad.

He has the distinction of holding fourteen solo shows and about seventy group shows all over India and abroad in Kirsten Kjaers Museum, Denmark 2001; Gallery Paialeh, Copenhagen, Denmark 2001; Cobra Gallery, Copenhagen, Denmark 1995; Vingsted Center, Denmark 1996 and 1999; Tao Art Gallery,

Bombay 2000; Shridharni Gallery, New Delhi 2000; Jehangir Art Gallery, Bombay 2001; Gallery Espace, New Delhi 1992; Lalit Kala Academy, Madras & New Delhi 1997; Minaz Art Gallery, Hyderabad 1999; ABC Gallery, Babaras 1995.

He has also participated in International Installation Workshop TIDE, Denmark 1996 and has work with renowned European Printmakers in Print making workshops in 1996 and 1999. He lives and works in Hyderabad.

❖

Iqbal Patni is a poet, artist and media personality. As a poet he is known for using simple words, pleasing rhythm and everyday language to communicate his thoughts effectively to the audiences. He has developed his own style of recital, which coupled with his sensuous voice brings out positive emotions and euphoric feeling in his listeners. His poetic talent has been appreciated and applied by some renowned names of the entertainment industry like A.R Rahman, Illayaraja, Anaida, Talat Aziz, Raj Kumar Rizvi etc.

Tasveer Ki Awaaz (The Voice of Images) is a unique concept created by Iqbal Patni by fusing the imagery of the artist with his poetic verses, where two diverse art forms—poetry and paintings—compliment each other. This unique concept was presented by Iqbal Patni at several prestigious Art Galleries like Tao Mumbai, Prince of Wales Museum, Mumbai and art festivals like Kala Ghoda, Mumbai, SAARC Artists Camp, Hyderabad, etc. The concept of *Tasveer Ki Awaaz*, when applied for showcasing fashion created magical effect on viewers. Popular fashion designers like Manish Malhotra, Wendell Rodricks, Gitanjali Kashyap, Krishna Mehta, Satya Paul and Vinita Pittei have showcased their collection using this concept where Poetry was blended with Fashion.

Lakshmi Devi Raj, gutsy, outspoken, and an untiring champion to the cause of communal harmony has organised several acts and street plays to revive the spirit of friendship and camaraderie which existed between Hindus and Muslims in the good old days in Hyderabad. Hailing from one of the oldest Hyderabadi families, her father was Doctor to the royal family of the prince and princess of Barar—the son and daughter-in-law of the seventh Nizam, HEH Mir Osman Ali Khan.

Lakshmi Devi Raj is the happiest when busy doing things to bring about change: setting up committees to improve the state of affairs, shooting letters of complaints to civic bodies, giving suggestions on city improvement to ministers over dinner, travelling to villages, setting up looms to revive the dying art of Kalamkari; the list goes on.

❖

Mithi Chinoy has valuable experience as a writer, having begun crafting life as a journalist in a film magazine and then moving on to a daily newspaper in Mumbai, India. She has also adapted a series of retold versions of children's classics for younger children, replete with a set of questions and activities. She has co-authored India's first fortnightly newspaper for children, *News N' Stuff.*

Since the past three years, she have been a ghost writer for umpteen e-books for clients in the US on a variety of subjects such as law, banking, pets, healthcare, photography and so on.

❖

Mohammad Ali Baig is a second generation theatre scion. As an ad-film maker, he has produced India's biggest adfilm; as a documentary film maker he has won the highest global award for his heritage film and as a theatre director he has made South India's biggest original musical production in Hindustani.

At an age when most youngsters would just come out of a film school or begin to assist senior film makers, Mohammad Ali Baig was already directing stalwarts in the world of ad-films. Before turning thirty he had already touched the awesome 300 plus adfilms mark for some of the top most global brands and Fortune 500 companies across seven cities in five countries and became the youngest director-on-board of India's pioneering public limited video production company in Bangalore.

While he is known for his adfilms which are epic in scale and larger-than-life in visual imagery, his documentary films on various social and heritage issues have won him the highest global awards internationally. He has won over twenty-four Advertising Awards, four National honours for his documentaries and two International Golds. Carrying on his father's legacy, he has given Hyderabad's theatre scene a new dimension with productions like *Taramati-A Legend of an Artist*, *His Exalted Highness* and *Reading Between the Lines* and having brought in some of the best theatre works from across the country to Hyderabad. His theatre revival movement has not just helped in reviving theatre in Hyderabad but has also aroused interest in the city's culture and heritage with his new genre of 'Heritage Theatre'. Not only that, he has pioneered a series of live theatre-conversations on stage titled 'Celebrating Theatre'. Mohammad Ali Baig hails from a renowned Hyderabadi family closely associated with the city's equestrian and cultural history.

❖

A former civil servant **Narendra Luther** is a well-known writer in Urdu and English. He is considered the best living authority on Hyderabad. Amongst his books are *Prince, Poet, Lover, Builder, Mohd. Quli Qutb Shah, the Founder of Hyderabad*; *Hyderabad—A Biography*; *The Nocturnal Court*; and *Raja Deen Dayal—Prince of Photography*. He is also a contributing author of a number of books and has written extensively on the subject. He has also produced some documentaries. Currently, he is working on a book on Secunderabad.

❖

Pratibha Karan was born in Mumbai. She grew up in Mumbai, Kolkata, Himachal Pradesh and Delhi. After post graduating in Economics from Lady Shri Ram College, she joined the Indian Administrative Service in 1967. She retired as Secretary to the Government of India in 2003. She married Vijay Karan, a Hyderabadi, and thus came in close touch with Hyderabadi Cuisine to which she took an abiding fondness. Pratibha Karan is the author of the book, *A Princely Legacy: Hyderabadi Cuisine.*

❖

G. Rajaraman was born on 10 March 1961 in Hyderabad. Son of eminent sports journalist N. Ganesan, he followed suit to pursue his passion for sports.

He joined the *The Hindu* as Sub-Editor in Chennai and the Press Trust of India as Sports Reporter in Hyderabad. Subsequently, he ventured to Delhi in July 1992, where he joined *The Pioneer* as a Senior Reporter/Sub-Editor (Sports). In 2001, he authored a book on match-fixing called *The Enemy Within.* He has also worked with the *Hindustan Times,* www.cricketnext. com, www.espnstar.com during his long and illustrious career. He joined the respected weekly magazine *Outlook* as Senior Special Correspondent in April 2005 and has recently begun conducting corporate training workshops, sharing knowledge gleaned over twenty-three years as a sports writer. He lives in New Delhi with his wife Sudha and daughter Priya and is now Sports Editor, *Samay,* Sahara India's National news channel.

❖

Rani Sarma has taught history in Delhi for twenty years and now shuttles between Visakhaptnam and Boston, USA. Actively involved in issues of heritage conservation, she strongly believes that heirtage should be conserved and protected in all its forms. She is a member of INTACH, Visakhapatnam Chapter. She is the author of *The Deodis of Hyderabad—A Lost Heritage* published by Rupa & Co.

❖

Sangita Reddy is the Managing Director of Apollo Health Street. Under her guidance, Apollo has become a leading offshore services firm and services some of the largest US payers and providers. She has been a pioneer in advocating the benefits of the global delivery model and has helped clients in overcoming the unique challenges of working with an offshore vendor. For more than twenty years, she has worked with providers and payers and has helped them optimise costs and improve service delivery. In addition to her leadership role at Apollo Health Street, she is also the Executive Director of the Apollo Hospitals Group, the third largest for-profit hospital group in the world.

❖

Shankar Krishnamurthy is the founder director of Fusion Hospitality Pvt. Ltd., chef owner of several restaurants, with Fusion 9 being the flagship restaurant. He started his career with The Oberoi School of Hotel Management as a Kitchen Trainee and went on to work with the Oberoi Hotels, Bombay for six years. The second phase of his career was an eight-year stint in Dubai, where he rose to become Executive Chef. The third phase of his career was an enriching experience of catering to visiting Heads of States and Royal families at The Soaltee Crowne Plaza in Kathmandu, Nepal.

He won a host of medals in several Salon Culinaire Competitions at Dubai during his tenure there. He also has the honour of leading the First Nepalese Culinary Team at the Singapore Food Asia.

Shankar Krishnamurthy is a visionary of sorts in the Food Industry and has contributed immensely to bring fine dining and international cuisine out of the thresholds of the luxury hotels in the twin cities of Hyderabad and Secunderabad, and make them easily accessible and affordable to the general public.

❖

Indukuri Syam Prasad Reddy is the Chairman & Managing Director of Indu Projects Limited, one of the fastest growing private sector engineering construction companies in India. In 2001, he branched out and started Indu Projects Limited, an end-to-end solutions provider in Infrastructure and Real Estate headquartered in Hyderabad with operations spread across the country.

Syam Prasad Reddy's contribution in the area of real estate and construction is immense. He has brought in professionalism to an otherwise unorganised industry and has actively contributed through forums such as TiE (The Indus Entrepreneurs) and FICCI (Federation of Indian Chambers of Commerce & Industry). For the knowledge and the vision Syam Prasad Reddy brings along, the Indian School of Business bestowed the honour of inviting him to join their Executive Board in 2008.

Syam Prasad Reddy is married to Sundari, a homemaker and they are blessed with two children, Sindhura and Siddharth.

❖

Vanaja Banagiri is the former editor of *Hyderabad Times*, the *Times of India*'s city edition. She has been associated with *Savvy*, *Society*, *Femina*, *Filmfare*, *Health & Nutrition* and the *Economic*

Times in various editorial capacities. She has also written for the *Sunday Observer, Cosmopolitan, Elle, Me* and *New Woman*. She won many awards for excellence during her journalistic career for her path breaking stories. At forty, she quit active journalism to pursue her long cherished dream of writing a book. Her debut novel *Butterflies and Barbed Wires* published by Rupa & Co was released in 2006. She also writes poetry. *Hyderabad Hazir Hai* is her second book. She lives in Hyderabad and is currently working on her third book—a psychological thriller.

Vijay Marur is a multi-faceted personality. He is a communications consultant, multimedia specialist, author, poet, features writer, actor, director and a professional voice over. He is also the winner of several awards for copywriting and Ad/Corporate filmmaking.

An alumni of Hyderabad Public School, Begumpet and Loyola College, Chennai, he subsequently dropped out of IIM Bangalore. He is married to an artist and HR consultant/soft skills trainer, has two daughters both of whom are studying communication and two dogs who don't need any such training.

❖

Aimed with a legacy of discipline, punctuality and hard work from her parents, **Vinita Pittie** found a comfortable and cushy balance in Hyderabad, where she relocated after her marriage. Though a housewife at heart, she has a small enterprise that allows her to translate her dreams into reality. Currently she lives in Hyderabad with her family, three cows and a dog.

5453